101 INCREDIBLE
GLUTEN-FREE
Recipes

JENNIFER BIGLER

CREATOR OF LIVING FREELY GLUTEN FREE

PAGE STREET
PUBLISHING CO.

PAGE STREET
PUBLISHING CO.

First published in 2020 by
Page Street Publishing Co.
27 Congress Street, Suite 105
Salem, MA 01970
www.pagestreetpublishing.com

Distributed by Macmillan, sales in Canada by The Canadian Manda Group.

24 23 22 21 20   1 2 3 4 5

ISBN-13: 978-1-62414-966-5
ISBN-10: 1-62414-966-9

Library of Congress Control Number: 2019942824

Cover and book design by Laura Benton for Page Street Publishing Co.
Photography by Jennifer Bigler
Photos on pages 6, 9, 11, 191 and 237 by j.petephotography

Printed and bound in China

Contents

Introduction

Going gluten-free is not easy at first. Through food, we all find comfort and joy. Having to eliminate dishes that you have been enjoying your entire life is not a good feeling. It can be intimidating, overwhelming and scary, yet sometimes you just need to take a leap. So many of us are suffering from celiac disease, a gluten allergy, gluten intolerance or autoimmune diseases that bring us to a gluten-free diet. I felt so lost when I first went gluten-free.

I remember eating nothing but fruit for my first week of being gluten-free, because I had no clue what was safe. Then, I became depressed and mourned the food that I missed. We are a family of food allergies. My son, daughter and I are allergic to gluten. My daughter and I are also lactose intolerant and now my son also has a corn allergy. My husband is along for the ride and went gluten-free because it made his life easier and actually made him feel better over time. He loves how he feels and how it helped with his shoulder arthritis.

To make matters worse, can you believe that I really didn't know much about cooking from scratch before going gluten-free? I was a product of the '80s and '90s, so most baked goods came from box mixes. I literally had to teach myself how to cook after going gluten-free.

I bought all the safe flours I could get my hands on and experimented until I made my own flour blend. Once I began making the foods we wanted and loved, I knew I needed to share the recipes with others who were dealing with the same food allergies. Having food allergies and doing all of the research is enough work. None of us wants to cook multiple meals to accommodate everyone. That is why I started my blog and created this book.

These recipes are for everyone regardless of whether they need to be gluten-free. These practical recipes are full of flavor and you'd never know they're gluten-free! I want to cook safe food for my family while inviting over our friends and family. I know they are going to love the dishes, and they do!

This book is full of comforting hearty dishes, lighter Whole30/Paleo dinners and delectable desserts that will have your non-gluten-free friends and family asking for them. I believe in the power of a family sitting with one another at the dinner table and enjoying a meal together.

My goal with this book is to give you the recipes you need to get through each day a little easier. I want you to get back in the kitchen and enjoy the foods that you are making with your friends and family. It's time to start Living Freely Gluten Free. Now, let's make some delicious food.

Ingredients to Know Before You Start

FLOURS

I always recommend using my own gluten-free, all-purpose flour blend (page 229) when making these recipes. That is what I used for every single recipe in this book. There are recipes that my readers have made using a 1:1 blend from the store, and their results have been slightly different. When you buy the flours used for my flour blend, I recommend Bob's Red Mill or Anthony's brand. I have found the most success from these two brands.

OILS

You will see in all the recipes that I most often use avocado oil and coconut oil. This is because they are incredibly clean oils with a high heating point. They are full of healthy fats, and that is what I look for when I am choosing ingredients. I use olive oil in recipes such as salad dressings, marinades or anything that isn't going to be heated. When purchasing avocado oil, I look for cold-pressed; the same for olive oil. For coconut oil, I buy unrefined organic. If you do not like the flavor of coconut, refined coconut oil has less of a coconut taste.

You can always use vegetable oil or your oil of choice for any recipe that calls for avocado oil. I sometimes use firm coconut oil in recipes such as piecrust. If the recipe does not need to be dairy-free, then I would suggest butter or a butter alternative.

POTATO STARCH, TAPIOCA STARCH, ARROWROOT STARCH AND CORNSTARCH

Starches are essential in gluten-free baking to get great flaky textures. All four of these starches can do the job; however, tapioca is my favorite for thickening soups, stews and so on. I have found that potato starch makes things too thick. Arrowroot starch is perfect for Paleo and grain-free diets. Cornstarch always works well and is the least expensive, but it is also typically GMO and my son has a corn allergy, so we avoid it at all costs.

RICE FLOURS

I have experimented with many rice flours while making my gluten-free all-purpose flour blend (page 229). My favorite brand is Anthony's. You can mostly find it at Amazon or Anthony's own website. My second favorite is Bob's Red Mill. Those are the only two brands at this moment that I can recommend with confidence.

XANTHAN GUM, GUAR GUM AND PSYLLIUM HUSK

These are binders and are essential in gluten-free baking. Gluten is what binds regular baked goods, and because we are removing that, we need something to help bind ingredients so they do not fall apart. I used xanthan gum for years and recently switched to guar gum. Xanthan gum is derived from corn, and guar gum is derived from the guar bean; I switched because of my son's corn allergy. I have found that I prefer the guar gum over xanthan gum. Psyllium husk is a great alternative if you do not tolerate gums or if you are eating a grain-free Paleo diet. Although it does not work as well as xanthan gum or guar gum, it gets the job done. There is a slight difference in texture from each binder, but when in doubt, xanthan gum is a great choice.

Manageable Main Dishes

Dinners as a family are so incredibly important for bonding and connection. I grew up with a single mom, so having that "family together feeling" is a top priority for me. When someone is singled out for a food allergy, sitting together for a meal can cause stress and anxiety. All these recipes are for the entire family—whether or not they are gluten- and dairy-free, they will enjoy all of these meals.

Your family is going to love the comforting Family-Style Lasagna (page 16), fresh Pesto Pasta (page 20) and easy Sheet Pan Steak Fajitas (page 36). My kids liked the Perfect Pizza Crust (page 60), Mama's Meaty Chili (page 39) and Juicy Garlic Burgers (page 24). When hosting friends and family, my go-tos are the Oven-Roasted Pork Loin (page 12), Rosemary Roasted Chicken (page 40) and Classic Sunday Pot Roast (page 27). Never make two separate dinners again. Grab a loved one and get in the kitchen together.

OVEN-ROASTED PORK LOIN

SERVES 8

PALEO & WHOLE30

RUB

1 tsp granulated garlic
¼ tsp freshly ground black pepper
1 tsp sea salt
1 tsp dried parsley
¼ tsp dried sage
1 tsp dried thyme
1 tsp dried rosemary
½ tsp paprika

1 (3- to 4-lb (1.4- to 1.8-kg) boneless pork loin
1 tbsp (15 ml) avocado oil
½ cup (120 ml) broth (any kind)
1 onion, quartered
10 cloves garlic
1 lb (455 g) carrots, peeled and cut into strips

This beautiful dish is full of juicy flavor. If you are looking to serve several people and want something that looks fabulous on the table, this recipe is it. The pork loin is rubbed with flavorful herbs and then browned beautifully. It is a healthy dish that my kids have been requesting often.

Preheat the oven to 400°F (200°C).

Prepare the rub: In a small bowl, combine all the rub ingredients and stir well. Generously rub the entire pork loin with the mixture.

Heat the oil over medium heat in either a Dutch oven or large skillet. (If you use a skillet, you will have to transfer it to a baking dish; I prefer a Dutch oven, if the roast will fit.) Add the pork to the oil and brown on both sides, about 4 minutes per side.

Remove the pork from the pan and set aside. Deglaze the pan with the broth, then turn off the heat.

If using a Dutch oven, add the onion, garlic and carrots to the pan and place the pork on top. Cover and place on the lowest rack in the oven. If you used a skillet to brown the pork, in a 9 x 13–inch (23 x 33–cm) baking dish, combine the onion, garlic and all the broth from the skillet, add the carrots and then place the pork on top. If your baking dish has a lid, cover; if not, cover with foil and place in the oven.

Roast for 1 hour, or until the pork has an internal temperature of 145°F (63°C). Allow to rest for 20 minutes, then slice and serve.

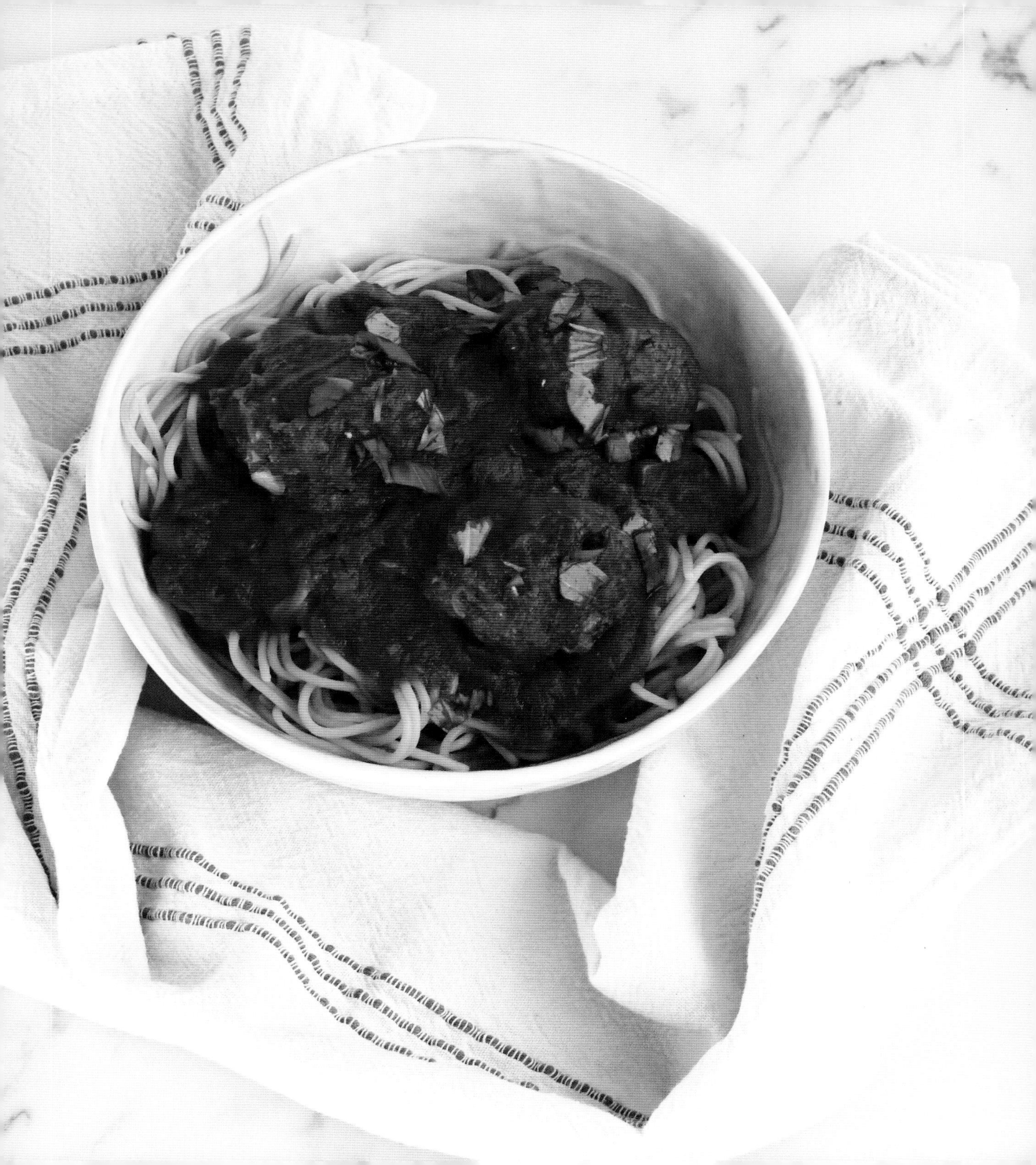

EGG-FREE ITALIAN MEATBALLS

MAKES 18 TO 24
MEATBALLS

PALEO & WHOLE30

2½ lb (1.1 kg) ground beef
½ onion, diced
1 green bell pepper, seeded and diced
2 tbsp (20 g) minced fresh garlic
2 tbsp (5 g) diced fresh basil, or 2 tsp (2 g) dried, plus 2 tbsp (5 g) diced basil for garnish
1 tsp sea salt
1 tsp dried parsley
½ tsp dried marjoram
½ tsp dried rosemary
¼ tsp freshly ground black pepper
1 tsp granulated garlic
5 cups (1.2 L) marinara sauce

Meatballs were something I always bought premade before going gluten-free. I started making meatballs out of necessity and I didn't like all the fuss that went into them, so I created these filler-free meatballs to make life easy and healthy. These are naturally Paleo and Whole30 compliant and since there are no breadcrumbs or eggs, you can taste all the fabulous flavors.

Preheat the oven to 400°F (200°C).

In a large bowl, combine all the ingredients, except the marinara sauce. Mix really well with a wooden spatula or your hands, to distribute the onion, bell pepper and all the seasonings evenly.

Form the mixture into meatballs the size of a golf ball. Place them in a large skillet and brown all sides over medium heat, about 2 minutes per side.

Transfer the meatballs to a 9 x 13–inch (23 x 33–cm) baking dish. Pour the marinara sauce on top of the meatballs. Cover the dish with foil and place in the oven.

Bake for 20 minutes. Serve on top of your favorite gluten-free noodles or spaghetti squash. You can also serve these as an appetizer. Garnish with fresh basil before serving.

MY TWO-CENTS
Browning the meatballs first is a very important step for keeping them intact because there are no binders in this recipe. You can brown ahead of time by panfrying them, allowing them to cool and then freezing them. They are not cooked all the way through by being panfried, so the oven step is very important on the day you will serve them, as it fully cooks the meatballs. When you're ready to bake them, take them out to thaw and then follow the directions above to bake in a 400°F (200°C) oven.

FAMILY-STYLE LASAGNA

SERVES 8

PALEO & WHOLE30 OPTION

CASHEW CREAM

1½ cups (210 g) raw cashews, soaked in water overnight

1 tbsp (8 g) nutritional yeast

½ tsp sea salt

2 tsp (10 ml) avocado oil

1 tsp granulated garlic

½ tsp dried parsley

½ tsp dried oregano

¾ cup (175 ml) coconut milk

LASAGNA

2 lb (905 g) ground beef

2 (25-oz [739-ml]) jars vegan spaghetti sauce

1 (10-oz [280-g]) box gluten-free lasagna noodles

1 (8-oz [225-g]) bag vegan mozzarella shreds (optional)

Lasagna is that go-to Sunday night dinner that brings everyone around the table. We never made this from scratch while I was growing up; it was always store-bought. After going gluten-free, I had to teach myself how to make lasagna, because I missed it so much. This recipe is rich and hearty, and my entire family loves it.

Prepare the cashew cream: In a blender, combine all the cashew cream ingredients and blend on high speed for 2 to 3 minutes, or until it has a nice creamy consistency. You may have to scrape the sides of the blender halfway through to mix thoroughly.

Preheat the oven to 400°F (200°C).

In a large skillet, brown the ground beef over medium heat.

Pour some of the spaghetti sauce onto the bottom of a 9 x 13–inch (23 x 33–cm) casserole dish. Add a layer of lasagna noodles, then more sauce and some of the meat, vegan mozzarella (if using) and cashew cream, spreading each layer to cover all the noodles. Repeat adding layers in the same order, ending with noodles. On the top, add any remaining sauce and a dollop of the cashew cream.

Bake, covered, for 50 minutes, then remove the cover and bake for an additional 10 minutes, or until the sauce is bubbling and the top is golden. Remove from the oven and allow to cool for 20 minutes before cutting.

MY TWO-CENTS

You can make this ahead and freeze before baking; it turns out amazing. I use the disposable aluminum baking pans that come with a lid for this. When ready to bake, allow it to thaw and then bake at 400°F (200°C) for 55 to 70 minutes, or until the middle is heated through and the sauce is bubbling.

To make this Paleo/Whole30, use thinly sliced zucchini in place of the lasagna noodles and decrease the baking time to 45 minutes.

SLOW-COOKED "FALL OFF THE BONE" RIBS

SERVES 4 OR 5

3 (15-oz [445-ml]) cans tomato sauce
2 tbsp (30 ml) cider vinegar
1 cup (225 g) light brown sugar
1 tsp onion powder
1½ tsp (5 g) granulated garlic
2 tsp (6 g) garlic salt
¼ cup (65 g) tomato paste
¼ cup (85 g) molasses
¼ tsp freshly ground black pepper
¼ tsp chili powder
3 tbsp (45 ml) pure maple syrup
¼ tsp crushed red pepper flakes
½ tsp smoked paprika
3 lb (1.4 kg) baby back ribs

Ribs are something that we did not used to eat during the winter months because we always cooked them on the barbecue grill. I created this recipe so that we could enjoy ribs during the colder months. Slow cooking them makes dinner easy, because I throw it together in the morning, and it's ready to go at dinnertime. The slow cooker also makes the ribs super-tender and marinates the sauce flavor into them.

Prepare the sauce: In a large saucepan, combine everything but the ribs and stir well. Bring to a light boil over medium heat, then lower the heat and simmer, stirring every 2 to 3 minutes, for 7 to 10 minutes, or until the sauce has come to a light boil and slightly thickened.

Cut the rack of ribs in half, place them in an 8-quart (7.6-L) slow cooker and smother them with the sauce. Cover with the lid and cook on LOW for 6 hours, or until the ribs are tender and ready to fall off the bone.

MY TWO-CENTS
This sauce doubles as a barbecue sauce. Feel free to make a batch for that purpose; it can be stored in the fridge for a week or so.

PESTO PASTA

SERVES 4

VEGAN, PALEO &
WHOLE30 OPTION

8 oz (225 g) gluten-free
spaghetti noodles or zoodles
(zucchini noodles)

PESTO

1½ cups (36 g) fresh basil leaves
1½ cups (45 g) spinach leaves
3 cloves garlic
1 tsp sea salt
Juice of ½ lemon
¼ cup (35 g) pine nuts
⅓ cup (80 ml) olive oil

I have fond memories of eating the pesto pasta that my nina made for me when I was a child. I have always loved pesto, and as an adult, I appreciate how easy it is to make. Traditional pesto is made with Parmesan cheese and basil. What with taking the dairy out, I added spinach for extra flavor and nutrients, and it balances out the flavor perfectly! I make this as a picnic lunch when I go to my favorite winery.

Boil the noodles according to the package directions or sauté zoodles with oil until tender.

Meanwhile, prepare the pesto: In a food processor, combine the basil, spinach, garlic, salt, lemon juice, pine nuts and a drizzle of the olive oil. Process for 4 to 5 minutes while continuing to pour in the remainder of the olive oil through the processor lid as you blend. Once the leaves are blended well and the mixture has a paste consistency, the pesto is ready.

Drain the noodles and transfer to a bowl, add the pesto to the noodles and toss to coat. You can serve this warm or cold.

MY TWO-CENTS
When choosing your spaghetti noodles, look for a gluten-free product made from quinoa or brown rice, for the best texture. If you can have corn, corn noodles work well, too.

LEMON–HERBED SALMON

SERVES 4

PALEO & WHOLE30

1½ lb (680 g) salmon fillet

2 tbsp (28 g) ghee or vegan butter, at room temperature

½ tsp sea salt

½ tsp granulated garlic

½ tsp chopped fresh parsley

½ tsp fresh or dried rosemary

¼ tsp dried sage

Sprinkle of freshly ground black pepper

1 lemon—juice half and slice the other half

Salmon is such a healthy and delicious meal, and it's incredibly easy to make. It cooks fast, so if you need something quick on a weeknight, salmon is the perfect choice. The ghee keeps this Paleo and Whole30 while still adding the fabulous buttery taste. Lemon gives it a slight citrus tang and, with all the herbs, the flavors meld together to create a light yet filling dish.

Preheat the oven to 400°F (200°C). Line a baking sheet with foil.

Lay the salmon on the foil, spread the ghee on top of the salmon, then sprinkle all the seasonings evenly on top. Squeeze the lemon juice over the salmon, then lay the lemon slices on top. Fold the foil up and over the salmon to cover all. Bake for 18 to 20 minutes, or until the salmon is flaky and light pink.

MY TWO-CENTS
You can use regular butter instead of the ghee or vegan butter, if this does not need to be dairy-free.

JUICY GARLIC BURGERS

SERVES 4

PALEO & WHOLE30 OPTION

BURGERS

1½ lb (680 g) ground beef
¼ cup (40 g) minced garlic
1 tsp granulated garlic
1 tsp sea salt
1 tsp dried parsley
¼ tsp freshly ground black pepper
1 tbsp (15 ml) coconut aminos

SPREAD

¼ cup (56 g) Simple From-Scratch Mayo (page 232)
1 tbsp (15 ml) ketchup
1 tbsp (15 g) sweet relish
Pinch of salt

TO ASSEMBLE

4 gluten-free buns
4 pieces lettuce
4 slices tomato
4 slices onion
4 slices avocado

There's nothing like a good ol' burger, and garlic is the perfect way to load it up with amazing flavor. This recipe is my favorite for an outdoor summer barbecue, or to just fry on the stovetop during the colder months, as directed here. The homemade spread takes this burger to another level.

In a bowl, combine the ground beef, minced garlic, granulated garlic, salt, parsley, pepper and coconut aminos. With your hands or a wooden spoon, mix the seasonings into the meat.

Divide the meat into 4 patties. Place in a large skillet, cook over medium heat for 1 minute and then flip. Cook them for a total of about 12 minutes, flipping every 2 minutes, so the meat cooks through without burning. This will give you well-done burgers, so adjust the time accordingly for your desired doneness.

Combine all of the spread ingredients and stir well.

Toast the buns and add some of the spread to the inside of both halves of each bun. Place a burger patty on each lower half, then add a piece of lettuce, slice of tomato, slice of onion and avocado. Add each top half and serve.

MY TWO-CENTS
You can always use gluten-free tamari in place of the coconut aminos.

I love serving this with the Ballpark Garlic Fries (page 90).

To make this Paleo/Whole30, omit the buns and wrap in lettuce.

CLASSIC SUNDAY POT ROAST

SERVES 5

2 tbsp (30 ml) avocado oil

1 (2-lb [905-g]) beef rump roast

½ cup (80 g) The Best Ever Gluten-Free All-Purpose Flour Blend (page 229)

1 onion, diced

2 tbsp (20 g) chopped fresh garlic

2 cups (475 ml) broth (any kind)

¾ tsp freshly ground black pepper

½ tsp paprika

½ tsp dried thyme

½ tsp dried rosemary

1 tsp dried parsley

1 tsp granulated garlic

1 tsp sea salt

2 bay leaves

2 cups (260 g) peeled and chopped carrots (about 6 carrots)

I grew up loving pot roast with mashed potatoes. My aunt Cheryl made the most delicious pot roast. I asked her how she made it, and this is my re-creation. To make it gluten-free, I replaced the flour in her recipe with my gluten-free blend and added my favorite herbs. Slow cooking it in a Dutch oven makes it incredibly tender and juicy.

Preheat the oven to 325°F (165°C).

In a Dutch oven, heat the oil over medium heat. Coat the roast with the flour blend and brown on all sides for about 3 minutes per side. Turn off the heat and add the onion, chopped garlic, broth, pepper, paprika, thyme, rosemary, parsley, granulated garlic, salt and bay leaves. Cover and bake for 2 hours.

At the 2-hour point, add the carrots. Cover and bake for an additional hour. Serve with Garlic Mashed Potatoes (page 97) and Perfect Popovers (page 133).

MY TWO-CENTS
To get a super-tender pot roast, a Dutch oven is recommended. However, you can brown the roast in a large skillet and transfer it to a lidded baking dish large enough to hold it, if needed.

BROCCOLI AND "CHEESE" SOUP

SERVES 4
VEGAN OPTION

2 tbsp (28 g) coconut oil
1 onion, diced
5 cloves garlic, diced
4 cups (364 g) washed and diced broccoli
2 carrots, peeled and diced
2 tbsp (28 g) vegan butter
¼ cup (40 g) The Best Ever Gluten-Free All-Purpose Flour Blend (page 229)
4 cups (960 ml) chicken broth
¼ cup (32 g) nutritional yeast
¾ tsp sea salt
¼ tsp freshly ground black pepper
½ tsp paprika
½ tsp dry mustard
3 cups (710 ml) coconut milk
½ to 1 cup (58 to 115 g) vegan cheddar shreds, plus more for topping (optional)

Nothing beats a warm bowl of amazing creamy broccoli and cheese soup. I used to order this at my favorite sandwich place. After going gluten- and dairy-free, I missed it terribly! You will love this comforting dish and it goes amazingly with my To-Die-For Dinner Rolls (page 134) or Bakery-Style French Bread (page 145).

In a large skillet, heat the coconut oil over medium heat. Add the onion, garlic, broccoli and carrots and sauté for 10 minutes, or until the broccoli is tender. Remove from the heat.

In a stockpot, melt the vegan butter over medium heat, then add the flour blend slowly, stirring constantly, to create a roux. You will know you have a roux when the mixture turns into something that looks like paste; it should be a blond color. Pour in the broth, slowly stirring at the same time, until it is all blended in. Add the nutritional yeast and stir. Add the sautéed veggies, salt, pepper, paprika and dry mustard. Lower the heat to medium-low and simmer for 6 to 8 minutes.

Add the coconut milk, 1 cup (240 ml) at a time, then simmer for 20 minutes, stirring often. If you like a creamy soup, remove half and blend it in a blender, then stir it back in. If you like it chunky, then leave it be. Add the vegan cheddar shreds (if using) and remove from the heat.

Serve with additional vegan cheddar shreds on top (if using).

MY TWO-CENTS

If you would like this recipe to be vegan, use vegetable broth instead of chicken broth.

The vegan shreds are a nice addition, but not necessary. I prefer Daiya brand cheddar shreds.

COLD WEATHER CLAM CHOWDER

SERVES 4

PALEO & WHOLE30 OPTION

4 slices bacon

1 onion, diced

1 tbsp (10 g) diced garlic

2 ribs celery, diced

16 oz (475 ml) clam juice

2 (6.5-oz [184-g]) cans clams, juice reserved

5 russet potatoes, peeled and cubed

½ tsp dried thyme

1 bay leaf

1 tsp salt

¼ tsp freshly ground black pepper

3 cups (710 ml) coconut milk, divided

2 tbsp (16 g) tapioca starch

2 tbsp (12 g) chopped green onions, for garnish

Clam chowder is a dish I remember enjoying with family during the cold months. My aunt Cheryl made my favorite clam chowder. When I decided to create a gluten- and dairy-free version, I asked her to help me. She told me how she made hers, and I swapped out the heavy cream for coconut milk, and the all-purpose flour for tapioca starch. It was an easy switch that turned out perfect. This is a bowl of comfort during the winter.

In a stockpot or Dutch oven, cook the bacon over medium heat until it begins to brown, flipping every 2 minutes. This should only take 4 to 6 minutes. Remove the bacon and set aside on a paper towel–lined plate, without draining the fat from the pot.

Add the onion, garlic and celery to the pot and sauté over medium heat for about 5 minutes. Add the clam juice and juice from the canned clams. To do this, simply open the cans and, leaving the top on, drain the juice into the pot, then set the clams aside.

Once the mixture begins to simmer, add the potatoes, thyme, bay leaf, salt and pepper. Allow the potatoes to cook until tender, 15 to 20 minutes, then transfer half of the potatoes to a blender (see note). Add 2 cups (475 ml) of the coconut milk and the tapioca starch to the blender. Blend on low speed for 45 seconds, then pour the mixture back into the pot, along with the remaining cup (240 ml) of coconut milk. Add the reserved clams, lower the heat to a low simmer and heat through, about 10 minutes. Remove the bay leaf. The chowder is then ready to serve. Garnish with the cooked bacon and green onions.

MY TWO-CENTS

If you prefer a chunky chowder, skip the step of blending the potatoes in a blender. Simply mix together the coconut milk and tapioca starch in a bowl and add it directly to the pot.

This recipe is Paleo and Whole30 compliant (if using Paleo-compliant bacon).

GINGER CHICKEN AND BROCCOLI

SERVES 4

PALEO & WHOLE30

3 tbsp (45 ml) avocado oil

1 lb (455 g) boneless, skinless chicken breast, sliced into bite-size pieces

1 head broccoli, washed and cut into florets

¼ cup (40 g) diced onion

1 tbsp (10 g) chopped fresh garlic

1 tsp grated fresh ginger

1 tsp sea salt

¼ tsp freshly ground black pepper

1 tsp granulated garlic

2 tbsp (30 ml) coconut aminos or gluten-free tamari

This is a lighter, healthier version of the dish I'd get when we'd order takeout. The fresh ginger gives it lots of flavor that complements the garlic. This is a great, easy weeknight meal and the leftovers are fabulous, too.

In a large skillet or wok, heat the avocado oil over medium heat. Add the chicken and sauté for 2 minutes. Flip and sauté for another 2 minutes.

Add the broccoli, onion, chopped garlic and ginger. Toss with your spatula. Add the salt, pepper, granulated garlic and coconut aminos. Lower the heat to medium-low, cover and simmer for 8 to 10 minutes, or until the broccoli is tender and the sauce has a slight boil. Remove from the heat and serve.

MY TWO-CENTS
You can serve this with the Cashew Fried Rice (page 35), or cauliflower rice to keep this Paleo/Whole30 compliant.

CASHEW FRIED RICE

Fried rice has been a takeout go-to for me; however, the sauces made it unsafe once I went gluten-free. Making it at home is incredibly easy and cheaper. The best part is you can use whatever you have in the fridge if you want to replace any ingredients.

2 tbsp (30 ml) avocado oil
1 tbsp (10 g) diced fresh garlic
½ cup (80 g) diced onion
1 cup (130 g) diced carrot
1 cup (150 g) peas
1 cup (165 g) pineapple chunks
1 cup (140 g) raw cashews
2 large eggs
3 cups (510 g) cooked white rice, cooled
2 tbsp (30 ml) gluten-free tamari
1 tsp sea salt
1 tsp granulated garlic
2 green onions, chopped, for garnish

In a large skillet or wok, heat the avocado oil over medium heat. Add the diced garlic, onion, carrot, peas, pineapple chunks and cashews. Sauté for 6 to 8 minutes, or until the onion is translucent and the pineapple is heated through.

Move the veggies to the side and add the eggs. Scramble the eggs into the mixture. Add the cooked rice, tamari, salt and granulated garlic. Sauté for about 4 minutes. Serve with the green onions on top.

MY TWO-CENTS
To make this Paleo/Whole30, simply use cauliflower rice in place of the regular rice and use coconut aminos instead of the tamari.

Omit the eggs to make this vegan.

SHEET PAN STEAK FAJITAS

SERVES 6
PALEO & WHOLE30

FAJITA SEASONING
¼ cup (30 g) chili powder
1 tbsp (18 g) sea salt
1 tbsp (7 g) paprika
1 tsp coconut sugar
2 tsp (5 g) onion powder
2 tsp (5 g) ground cumin
1 tsp granulated garlic

FAJITA
2 bell peppers, seeded and cut into strips
1 large onion, sliced
1 lb (455 g) flank steak, cut into thin strips
¼ cup (60 ml) avocado oil
¼ cup (36 g) fajita seasoning

TO ASSEMBLE
12 gluten-free tortillas (see page 146 for homemade)
Avocado, for garnish
Fresh cilantro, for garnish

Fajitas are something I make often, but I always cooked them on the stovetop. This is so much easier and faster, and the taste is incredible. The homemade seasoning coats every piece of steak and vegetables to give every bite a burst of flavor. I often eat it straight out of the pan without it even making it to a tortilla, because it is irresistible.

Preheat the oven to 400°F (200°C).

In a small bowl, combine all the seasoning ingredients and stir well. The seasoning can be made ahead of time and stored in an airtight container to use later.

In a medium-sized bowl, combine the bell peppers, onion and steak. Drizzle with the avocado oil and then sprinkle in ¼ cup (36 g) of the fajita seasoning, 1 tablespoon (9 g) at a time, stirring well in between each sprinkle to coat everything with the seasoning.

Transfer the steak mixture to a baking sheet and bake for 12 to 15 minutes. Remove the sheet from the oven and build your fajitas with the tortillas, avocado and cilantro.

MY TWO-CENTS
These are excellent as leftovers the next day. To reheat, drizzle a little oil into a skillet and heat over medium heat for 4 to 5 minutes, or until heated through. These are also perfect warm or cold on top of greens as a salad the next day.

MAMA'S MEATY CHILI

SERVES 4

WHOLE30 OPTION

1 tsp avocado oil

2 tbsp (20 g) chopped garlic

1 medium-sized onion, diced

2 lb (905 g) ground beef

1 tsp ground cumin

2 tsp (5 g) dried parsley

2 tsp (3 g) dried basil

1½ tbsp (11 g) chili powder

1 tsp sea salt

¼ tsp freshly ground black pepper

½ cup (120 ml) tomato sauce

1 (15-oz [425-g]) can kidney beans, drained

2 (15-oz [425-g]) cans black beans, drained

2 (14.5-oz [411-g]) cans diced tomatoes, undrained

I have been making this chili since we first went gluten-free. It is a crowd-pleaser that my entire family loves, especially my children. It is perfect for a cold winter's night, or to top your hot dogs, nachos and French fries. This recipe has become a tradition for Halloween as well. I invite all of my family over and double or triple this batch and feed everyone before trick-or-treating.

In a large pot, heat the avocado oil over medium heat. Add the garlic and onion and cook until the onion is translucent, 3 to 4 minutes. Add the beef and sprinkle with the cumin, parsley, basil, chili powder, salt and pepper. Brown the meat, 7 to 8 minutes. Once the meat is cooked, add the tomato sauce, beans and diced tomatoes. Bring to a simmer and cover. Cook, stirring every 10 minutes, for about 45 minutes, or until the beans are tender.

MY TWO-CENTS

To make this Whole30, replace the beans with 5 cups (665 g) of diced raw sweet potato.

Alternatively, you can make this in an Instant Pot: Combine the onions, garlic and meat mixture, sauté and brown on the sauté setting, then add the beans or sweet potatoes and tomatoes, tomato sauce and stir. Cook on the chili/meat setting for 20 minutes and that's it!

ROSEMARY ROASTED CHICKEN

SERVES 4

PALEO & WHOLE30

1 (2½- to 3-lb [1.1- to 1.4-kg]) chicken

1 tsp sea salt

1 tsp granulated garlic

¼ tsp freshly ground black pepper

1½ tsp (2 g) dried rosemary

2 tsp (10 ml) avocado oil

½ onion, sliced

4 sprigs rosemary

I started serving whole roasted chickens shortly after doing my first Whole30. I loved how you can reuse so many parts of the chicken for other things. I honestly think it is one of the most beautiful dishes to serve for guests when you lay it on a platter with some potatoes and carrots. This healthy dish is always a crowd-pleaser.

Preheat the oven to 350°F (180°C).

Place your chicken on a roasting pan, breast side up. Remove all the giblets, tip the carcass to drain any liquid out of it and pat dry with a paper towel. Rub the salt, granulated garlic, pepper and dried rosemary all over the chicken. Drizzle with the avocado oil. Stuff the chicken with the onion and rosemary sprigs.

Place, uncovered, in the oven. After 45 minutes, remove the bird and tilt it slightly to remove any excess liquid inside the carcass. Place the bird back in the oven. After roasting for 90 minutes total, check the internal temperature in the meaty part of the thigh; it should be 165°F (74°C) when the chicken is cooked through. Once the thigh reaches that temperature, remove from the oven and serve.

MY TWO-CENTS

I made the mistake of not tipping the bird and removing the excess liquid the first time I made this. It caused the bird to be underdone inside and overcooked on the outside.

Feel free to add extra flavors, such as carrots or apples, into the bird when stuffing.

RAINY DAY VEGETABLE SOUP

SERVES 5

VEGAN

I created this soup because I was in need of a super-healthy easy dinner that tasted amazing. I wanted something low in calories but full of goodness. This recipe is one of the top five most popular recipes on my blog, and for good reason.

2 tbsp (30 ml) avocado oil

2 cups (320 g) diced onion

2 tbsp (20 g) chopped fresh garlic

3 cups (372 g) diced zucchini (4 medium-size zucchini)

1 potato, chopped into bite-size pieces

3 cups (396 g) frozen mixed vegetables

1 (14-oz [400-g]) can stewed tomatoes

1 (14-oz [400-g]) can diced tomatoes

6 cups (1.4 L) chicken or vegetable broth

1 tsp granulated garlic

½ sprig fresh rosemary, or 1 tsp dried

2 tbsp (8 g) chopped fresh parsley, or 1½ tsp (2 g) dried

1 tsp dried thyme

1½ tsp (9 g) sea salt

½ tsp freshly ground black pepper

2 bay leaves

In a large stockpot, heat the avocado oil over medium heat. Add the onion and garlic, then sauté for 3 minutes. Add the zucchini, potato and mixed vegetables. Sauté for 5 more minutes. Add the canned tomatoes, broth and all the seasonings. Bring to a boil. Lower the heat to low and simmer, covered, stirring every 5 minutes or so, for 25 to 30 minutes, or until the carrots and potato are tender. Remove the bay leaves. Remove from the heat and serve. Enjoy!

MY TWO-CENTS

You cannot go wrong with this recipe and it can become a "whatever is left in the fridge" dish. I have left out the zucchini and added extra potato. Customize it however you would like.

You can also make this in an Instant Pot by following the directions above and then cooking it on the soup setting for 25 minutes.

GRANDMA OLGA'S CABBAGE STEW

SERVES 5
PALEO & WHOLE30

3 tbsp (45 ml) avocado oil
1 onion, diced
6 cloves garlic, diced
1½ lb (680 g) beef stew meat, such as chuck or round steak
4 cups (960 ml) beef broth
6 carrots, peeled and diced
6 potatoes, peeled and cubed
1 bay leaf
1 tsp paprika
½ tsp dried parsley
½ tsp granulated garlic
¾ tsp salt
¼ tsp freshly ground black pepper
5 to 6 cups (445 to 534 g) washed and chopped cabbage

Stew is one of our cold-weather favorites. While I was growing up, my grandma would make her stew with cabbage in it. As a parent, you are always looking for ways to sneak in a few more veggies and this is the perfect way. The cabbage adds another element of flavor and texture, plus it's more filling—when feeding a family on a budget, I am always looking for frugal ways to fill up everyone's belly.

Heat a Dutch oven or large pot over medium heat, then add the oil. Sauté the onion and garlic for 2 minutes. Add the stew meat and brown for about 6 minutes, stirring every 30 seconds.

Add the broth, carrots, potatoes, bay leaf, paprika, parsley, granulated garlic, salt and pepper. Bring to a boil, then cover and lower the heat to medium-low. Cook for 20 minutes, then add the cabbage. Cover and cook for 10 to 12 more minutes. Turn off the heat and let it sit for 5 minutes, then serve.

ORANGE CHICKEN

Oh my goodness, orange chicken is such a treat, but finding one that is gluten-, dairy- and corn-free for our family is absolutely impossible. Luckily, this recipe is pretty easy to make and tastes amazing. I often have to double it, because we love it that much.

SERVES 4

PALEO & WHOLE30 OPTION

SAUCE

¾ cup (170 g) light brown sugar

1 cup (240 ml) fresh orange juice

⅓ cup (80 ml) gluten-free tamari or coconut aminos

¼ cup (60 ml) white wine vinegar

½ tsp sea salt

Zest of 1 orange

½ tsp granulated garlic

½ tsp ground ginger

½ tsp red pepper flakes

2 tbsp (30 ml) water

1 tsp tapioca starch

CHICKEN

3 large eggs

½ cup (64 g) tapioca starch

½ cup (80 g) The Best Ever Gluten-Free All-Purpose Flour Blend (page 229)

1½ lb (680 g) boneless, skinless chicken breast, cut into bite-size pieces

1 cup (240 ml) avocado oil or (225 g) coconut oil, for frying

2 green onions, for garnish

Prepare the sauce: In a large saucepan, combine the brown sugar, orange juice, tamari, vinegar, salt, orange zest, granulated garlic, ginger and red pepper flakes. Heat over medium-low heat for about 4 minutes. In a small bowl, whisk together the water and tapioca starch, then add the mixture to the saucepan. Bring to a boil, lower the heat to a simmer and cook, stirring once every minute, for 15 to 20 minutes.

Meanwhile, fry the chicken: In a shallow bowl, whisk the eggs. In a separate shallow bowl, whisk together the tapioca starch and the flour blend. Dip the chicken pieces into the eggs and then into the flour mixture, coating the chicken on all sides. In a large skillet, heat the oil over medium heat. Place the chicken into the hot oil and fry for about 4 minutes per side. Once they are done, place the cooked pieces on a paper towel–lined plate.

Once the sauce is done, pour it over the chicken, or even add the chicken to the pan with the sauce if it is large enough and toss the chicken into the sauce.

Garnish with the green onions.

MY TWO-CENTS

Serve this with the Cashew Fried Rice (page 35).

If you are Paleo/Whole30, be sure to use coconut aminos or coconut sugar in place of the brown sugar, and a diet-compliant orange juice (you could simply juice an orange or two). You will also need to replace the gluten-free all-purpose flour with tapioca starch.

SHREDDED PINEAPPLE PORK TACOS

MAKES 15 TO 18 TACOS

PALEO & WHOLE30 OPTION

1 (20-oz [567-g]) can pineapple chunks in juice, undrained

1 (4-oz [113-g]) can diced green chiles

1 medium-sized onion, diced

3 lb (1.4 kg) boneless pork shoulder

1 tsp sea salt

¼ tsp freshly ground black pepper

½ tsp granulated garlic

¼ tsp cayenne pepper

½ tsp chili powder

½ tsp ground cumin

15 to 18 gluten-free tortillas (see page 146 for homemade), warmed

2 cups (178 g) shredded cabbage

These flavorful tacos are the perfect easy meal to throw together in the morning and have ready to go when you get home. The sweet with the savory makes it the perfect weeknight taco.

In an 8-quart (7.6-L) slow cooker, combine the pineapple chunks and their juice with the green chiles and onion.

Place the pork shoulder on top. Season the pork with the salt, black pepper, granulated garlic, cayenne, chili powder and cumin.

Cook on low for 8 hours or on medium for 6 hours, then shred the pork with a fork and knife.

Use a slotted spoon to pick up the pineapple pork and place it on your warmed tortillas. Garnish with the shredded cabbage.

MY TWO-CENTS
This shredded pineapple pork is naturally Paleo/Whole30 on its own. You can use it in a salad to keep it Whole30, or use grain-free tortillas for Paleo.

HEARTY HOMESTYLE CHICKEN POTPIE

SERVES 8

2 batches Easy Roll-Out Pie Dough (page 137)

3 potatoes

2 tbsp (30 ml) avocado oil

1 onion, diced

2 cups (264 g) frozen mixed vegetables

3 tbsp (42 g) vegan butter

1 cup (240 ml) coconut milk

¼ cup (32 g) tapioca starch

2 cups (475 ml) chicken broth

1½ lb (680 g) boneless, skinless chicken thighs, cooked and shredded

½ tsp dried thyme

1 tsp dried parsley

1 tsp sea salt

½ tsp freshly ground black pepper

When I created this recipe, a lot of elements had to be switched out to make it gluten- and dairy-free. First was the piecrust, then I had to use vegan butter and coconut milk in place of the dairy. To thicken it, I used tapioca starch. All of these switches created the perfect chicken potpie. I knew it was a winner when my picky father came over for dinner and he went back for seconds and thirds. He is not gluten-free and really enjoyed this dish.

Roll out each pie dough to 11 inches (28 cm) in diameter and place 1 dough disk in a 9-inch (23-cm) pie dish. Gently press down to fit it to the dish and shape the edges.

Preheat the oven to 350°F (180°C). Peel the potatoes, poke holes in them using a fork, cover them with a paper towel and microwave for 3 minutes on HIGH. Remove from the microwave, cut into bite-size cubes and set aside.

In a large skillet, heat the avocado oil over medium heat and sauté the onion for 5 minutes. Add the mixed vegetables and sauté for 10 minutes. Remove the veggies from the pan. Add the vegan butter to the pan and allow it to melt. Add the coconut milk and tapioca starch, stirring constantly while adding. Add the chicken broth, 1 cup (240 ml) at a time, and cook for 6 minutes, stirring every 30 seconds. Add the veggies back to the pan along with the potatoes, chicken, thyme, parsley, salt and pepper. Cook for 2 to 4 minutes, or until the mixture has slightly thickened. Pour into the dough-lined pie dish.

Top with the second piecrust, cut around the edges and pinch the two crusts around the rim to secure them closed. Slit the top with six 2-inch (5-cm) slits. Bake for 45 minutes, or until the crust has slightly browned and the vegetables in the pie are tender. Remove from the oven and allow the potpie to sit for 15 to 20 minutes before serving.

MY TWO-CENTS

If you don't feel like making pie dough, you can make this without the piecrust in a baking dish and use From-Scratch Biscuits (page 171) minus their gravy, on top. Bake at 350°F (180°C) for 20 minutes.

SATISFYING PORK STEW

We eat a lot of soups and stews in the winter. I wanted to try something different, so I decided to make a spin-off of my traditional beef stew and created a pork stew. It's a filling and flavorful meal that goes great with my Perfect Popovers (page 133) or Bakery-Style French Bread (page 145).

SERVES 5

PALEO & WHOLE30

2 tbsp (30 ml) avocado oil
1 onion, diced
2 tbsp (20 g) minced fresh garlic
6 carrots, peeled and diced
2 ribs celery, diced
1 cup (100 g) green beans
3 cups (710 ml) broth
1 (2-lb [905-g]) pork roast, cubed into bite-size pieces
1 tsp sea salt
¼ tsp freshly ground black pepper
½ tsp granulated garlic
1 tsp paprika
1 tsp dried parsley
1 tsp dried thyme
2 bay leaves

In a Dutch oven, heat the avocado oil over medium heat. Add the onion and minced garlic and sauté for 2 minutes. Add the carrots, celery and green beans and sauté for 3 minutes. Add the broth and pork. Stir well and add the salt, pepper, granulated garlic, paprika, parsley, thyme and bay leaves. Cover, lower the heat to medium-low and cook for 35 minutes, or until the pork is tender. Remove the bay leaves before serving.

MY TWO-CENTS

Feel free to add extra veggies, such as cabbage, peas or anything you have in the fridge.

I typically use vegetable broth for this recipe, but any broth will do.

ITALIAN EGGPLANT "PARMESAN"

SERVES 6

CASHEW CREAM

1½ cups (210 g) raw cashews, soaked in water overnight

¾ cup (175 ml) coconut milk

1 tbsp (8 g) nutritional yeast

½ tsp sea salt

2 tsp (10 ml) avocado oil

1 tsp granulated garlic

½ tsp dried parsley

½ tsp dried oregano

2 large eggs

1 cup (160 g) The Best Ever Gluten-Free All-Purpose Flour Blend (page 229)

1 cup (115 g) gluten-free breadcrumbs

1½ tsp (9 g) sea salt

2 tsp (6 g) granulated garlic

¼ tsp freshly ground black pepper

1 tsp dried basil

1½ cups (355 ml) avocado oil

2 eggplants, washed and sliced ¼ inch (6 mm) thick

3 cups (710 ml) vegan spaghetti sauce

2 fresh basil leaves, chopped, for garnish

This rich and decadent adaptation of eggplant Parmesan reminds me of the one that I used to order out. It is first fried for the perfect crispy edges and then layered in cashew cream. I smother it in sauce and bake it to be bubbly golden brown. You can eat it alone, but it's always fabulous with noodles.

Prepare the cashew cream: Drain the cashews and place them in a blender along with the coconut milk, nutritional yeast, salt, avocado oil, granulated garlic, parsley and oregano. Blend on high speed for about 3 minutes, or until creamy. You can add a few more splashes of coconut milk, if needed.

Preheat the oven to 400°F (200°C).

In a bowl or pie dish, beat the eggs well with a whisk or fork. In a separate bowl or pie dish, combine the flour blend, breadcrumbs, salt, granulated garlic, pepper and basil. Stir well.

In a large skillet, heat the avocado oil over medium heat. Dip the eggplant slices in the eggs, then the breadcrumb mixture, coating each slice entirely with the breadcrumb mixture. Once the oil is hot, working in batches, add the eggplant to the pan. Cook for 2 to 3 minutes on one side, then flip and cook for 2 more minutes. Once cooked, transfer to a paper towel–lined plate. Repeat until all the eggplant is cooked, adding more oil for cooking, if needed.

Pour some of the spaghetti sauce into the bottom of a large baking dish, then layer the bottom of the dish with some of the eggplant. Generously spoon cashew cream over the eggplant layer, then drizzle more spaghetti sauce on top. Continue this pattern until all the eggplant is in the baking dish. Bake for 20 minutes.

Remove from the oven, sprinkle with freshly chopped basil and serve.

MY TWO-CENTS

Some store-bought sauces can contain dairy, so make sure to check the ingredients if you are dairy-free.

You can use vegetable oil if you would like, instead of avocado oil.

EASY CHEESY BAKED ZITI

SERVES 6

This creamy pasta bake is the perfect comfort food. You will love the layers of noodles with cashew cream sauce. This is one of my kids' favorites, and I can't blame them, because I love it, too.

1 lb (455 g) ground beef
1 tsp sea salt
¼ tsp freshly ground black pepper
1 tsp granulated garlic
1 tsp dried basil
1 (24-oz [710-ml]) jar vegan pasta sauce
1 (8-oz [225-g]) box gluten-free ziti or penne noodles
Nonstick spray
1 batch Cashew Cream (pages 16 or 55)
1 cup (115 g) vegan mozzarella shreds (optional)

In a large skillet, brown the ground beef over medium heat and add the salt, pepper, granulated garlic and basil. Cook until the meat is browned and cooked through, 5 to 7 minutes. Add the pasta sauce and remove from the heat.

Preheat the oven to 350°F (180°C).

Boil the noodles according to the package directions, then drain and add the noodles to the meat mixture. Spray a 9 x 13–inch (23 x 33–cm) baking dish with nonstick spray and layer in half of the noodle mixture, half of the cashew cream, the remaining noodle mixture, the remaining cashew cream and the vegan mozzarella shreds (if using). Bake for 20 minutes, or until the cashew cream has turned golden brown, and the sauce is boiling.

MY TWO-CENTS
Gluten-free ziti noodles can be hard to find and that is why I listed penne as an option. Truly, any noodle shape will do the job.

STEAK
WITH SAUTÉED ONIONS AND MUSHROOMS

Steak is something we eat often because it is easy and the kids like it. I was getting tired of the same old panfried steak and decided to boost the taste with a rub and to then sauté onions and mushrooms in the seasoning. This really brought the steak to life and added some much needed flavor.

SERVES 4

PALEO & WHOLE30 OPTION

STEAK RUB

¾ tsp chili powder

1 tsp paprika

1 tsp granulated garlic

1 tsp sea salt

¼ tsp freshly ground black pepper

¾ tsp ground cumin

½ tsp onion powder

1 tsp dried sage

2 lb (905 g) top sirloin steak

3 tbsp (45 ml) avocado oil

3 tbsp (42 g) vegan butter or ghee

1 onion, sliced

8 oz (225 g) sliced mushrooms

In a small bowl, whisk together all the rub ingredients. Reserving 1 teaspoon of the rub, rub the steaks generously with the rest of the mixture.

In a large skillet, heat the avocado oil over medium heat. Place the steaks in the pan, cook for 2 minutes and flip. Continue to cook for 2 minutes per side for a total of about 12 minutes. Use a meat thermometer to check the temperature, or cut the steak in half to check doneness. Medium-well done should be 150 to 155°F (66 to 68°C). Increase or decrease the cooking time to achieve your desired doneness.

Once the steaks are done, transfer them to a plate and cover the plate with foil to keep them warm.

Add the vegan butter to the hot pan you used for the steaks. Once melted, add the onion and mushrooms. Sprinkle them with the reserved teaspoon of steak rub. Sauté for 10 to 12 minutes over medium-low heat and serve on top of the steak.

PERFECT PIZZA CRUST

MAKES ONE
12" TO 14"
(30- TO 35-CM)
PIZZA

VEGAN OPTION

2½ tbsp (30 g) active dry yeast

1 tbsp (13 g) sugar

1½ cups (355 ml) warm water (110°F [43°C]), divided

2½ cups (400 g) The Best Ever Gluten-Free All-Purpose Flour Blend (page 229)

1 tsp xanthan gum

½ tsp sea salt

½ tsp dried basil

½ tsp granulated garlic

2 tbsp (30 ml) avocado oil

TO CREATE A PIZZA

½ cup (120 ml) marinara sauce

1 cup (about 120 g) of your favorite toppings (I used sliced vegan cheese, salami, pepperoni, bell peppers and mushrooms)

Pizza is so hard to get right. I have been playing around with pizza dough for years, and I have had a few recipes. This time, I wanted something that is fluffy with good texture. My kids really went crazy for this dough. The best part is it's made with easy-to-find ingredients and it's vegan!

Preheat the oven to 350°F (180°C). Line a baking sheet with parchment paper.

Activate the yeast: In a small bowl, add the yeast and sugar to 1 cup (240 ml) of the warm water and give it a stir. When it doubles in size, 6 to 8 minutes, it is ready.

In a stand mixer fitted with the paddle attachment, combine the flour blend, xanthan gum, salt, basil and granulated garlic. Mix on low speed for 30 seconds, then add the activated yeast and blend on medium-low speed for 1 minute, scraping the sides of the bowl halfway through. With the mixer still on, add the remaining ½ cup (115 ml) of warm water and the avocado oil. Allow it to blend in and then turn off the mixer.

Place the dough on the prepared baking sheet. Use wet hands to shape the dough to 12 to 14 inches (30 to 35 cm) in diameter. You can flatten it and smooth it; just keep your hands wet.

Bake the dough for 15 minutes and remove from the oven.

To create a pizza: Add the marinara sauce and your choice of toppings. Bake for an additional 8 to 12 minutes, or until the cheese has a slight melt and the toppings are cooked through, and serve.

MY TWO-CENTS
This dough is naturally vegan, so this is the perfect dish to serve to vegan guests. Simply leave out the meat and add additional veggies.

TURMERIC SAGE FRIED CHICKEN

SERVES 5

PALEO

1½ cups (337 g) coconut oil
1½ cups (192 g) tapioca starch
2½ tsp (15 g) sea salt
1 tbsp (2 g) dried sage
1 tbsp (7 g) ground turmeric
1 tbsp (9 g) granulated garlic
¼ tsp freshly ground black pepper
1 tsp paprika
1 tsp chili powder
½ tsp cayenne pepper
3 lb (1.4 kg) chicken drumsticks

Fried chicken is something I loved while growing up. I make it often, but I wanted a fun and tasty spin on it, and that is exactly what I got by adding the turmeric and sage. This juicy fried chicken is healthy and full of fabulous flavor.

In a large skillet, heat the coconut oil over medium heat. Once the temperature reaches 300°F (150°C), it is ready for frying.

Meanwhile, in a large ziplock bag, combine all the remaining ingredients, except the drumsticks. Seal the bag and use your hands to blend the seasonings into the starch. Add 4 drumsticks at a time, seal the bag and toss them around in the mixture to coat on all sides. Working in batches, place the coated drumsticks into the hot oil. Cook each drumstick, turning every 1½ to 2 minutes, for a total of 12 to 15 minutes. Once the chicken is done, transfer to a cooling rack set over a paper towel–lined baking sheet to absorb the excess oil.

MY TWO-CENTS
If you are not into drumsticks, then use boneless, skinless chicken thighs cut into 1-inch (2.5-cm) strips. You might need to adjust the cooking time. Cook for about 4 minutes on each side.

You can also use any oil in place of the coconut oil, but make sure it is one that is safe for high temperatures.

HOT BRAISED PRAWNS

SERVES 4
PALEO OPTION

2 tbsp (30 ml) avocado oil

2 tbsp (20 g) diced garlic

¼ cup (31 g) diced water chestnuts

¼ cup (60 ml) ketchup

1 tbsp (15 ml) chili paste

2 tsp (10 ml) ginger paste

2 tbsp (30 ml) coconut aminos or gluten-free tamari

¼ cup (60 ml) red wine

2 tbsp (30 ml) white vinegar

¼ tsp salt

1 lb (455 g) shrimp, peeled and deveined

Diced green onions, for garnish

My husband and I have a favorite Chinese restaurant in California that accommodates our gluten allergy, and I have been ordering the hot braised prawns there for more than a decade. When we lived in Washington, I craved them so badly. Traditional hot braised prawns have a few more steps to them, but I figured out how to make this recipe easy. They are so simple that you could make this on a weeknight.

In a large skillet or wok, heat the avocado oil over medium heat and add the garlic, water chestnuts, ketchup, chili paste, ginger paste, coconut aminos, red wine, vinegar and salt. Stir to combine and bring to a light simmer. Add the shrimp, cover and cook for 3 minutes. Flip the shrimp and cook for 2 more minutes. Remove from the heat and serve garnished with the green onions.

MY TWO-CENTS
If you can find Paleo ketchup, you could make these Paleo and serve with cauliflower rice for the perfect healthy dinner.

MACADAMIA COCONUT-CRUSTED MAHI-MAHI

SERVES 5 OR 6

¾ cup (101 g) macadamia nuts
¾ cup (64 g) shredded coconut
½ cup (80 g) The Best Ever Gluten-Free All-Purpose Flour Blend (page 229)
2 large eggs, beaten
3 tbsp (21 g) coconut flour
¾ cup (96 g) tapioca starch
5 or 6 mahi-mahi fillets

PINEAPPLE SALSA

2 tomatoes, diced
½ red onion, diced
1 cup (165 g) diced pineapple
1 tbsp (3 g) chopped fresh cilantro
Sprinkle of sea salt
Sprinkle of freshly ground black pepper

5 oz (140 g) baby arugula, for serving (optional)

My husband and I traveled to Monterey once for our anniversary and we ate at a cute seaside restaurant. I wanted the macadamia-crusted mahi-mahi, but it wasn't gluten-free. I was determined to go home and create an even better version to enjoy. I did this by making a mixture with my gluten-free, all-purpose flour blend (page 229), coconut and crushed macadamia nuts. The tapioca starch makes it have a crispy texture, and the pineapple salsa gives this dish a fun and tropical flavor.

Preheat the oven to 425°F (220°C). Line a baking sheet with parchment paper.

In a food processor, combine the macadamia nuts and coconut and process until the mixture has a very crumbly texture with no chunks, about 30 seconds.

Line up 3 shallow bowls or pie dishes. In the first, place the flour blend. In the second, place the beaten eggs. In the third, stir together the coconut flour, tapioca starch and macadamia mixture. Coat each fillet by dipping it first into the flour blend, then into the eggs, then into the macadamia mixture. Then, place the breaded fish on the prepared baking sheet.

Bake for 18 to 22 minutes, or until the crust is golden brown and the fish is flaky.

While the fish bakes, prepare the salsa: In a medium-sized bowl, stir together all the salsa ingredients.

Serve the fish on a bed of arugula, if desired, with the salsa on top.

MY TWO-CENTS
The mahi-mahi coating in this recipe is the same as for the Coconut Prawns (page 82). I like to double the coating recipe and make both dishes at the same time.

Mouthwatering Munchies

Everyone deserves delicious appetizers for game day, gatherings and just because they are awesome. I love to host, and these are the dishes that I am serving to my friends and family. All of these recipes are for foods that I loved before going gluten-free. I may not be able to go to a restaurant and order onion rings or fried zucchini anymore, but these finger foods are so mouthwatering that I don't even care! Make three or four of these and invite your friends over. I have also eaten the entire batch of cauliflower wings by myself—they are that incredible!

DINER-STYLE ONION RINGS

SERVES 6

2 large onions
1¼ cups (200 g) The Best Ever Gluten-Free All-Purpose Flour Blend (page 229)
¾ cup (83 g) gluten-free panko-style breadcrumbs
½ tsp salt
½ tsp granulated garlic
¼ tsp freshly ground black pepper
2 large eggs
1 cup (240 ml) coconut milk, plus more if needed
1½ cups (337 g) coconut oil

CAMPFIRE SAUCE

½ cup (115 g) Simple From-Scratch Mayo (page 232)
½ cup (120 ml) barbecue sauce
3 dashes of hot sauce
¼ tsp red pepper flakes
1 tsp coconut aminos
Pinch of salt
Pinch of freshly ground black pepper
Pinch of granulated garlic

These are the onion rings you have been craving and missing. They are fried to perfection in a simple batter, and the campfire dipping sauce takes them to the next level. My kids have been wanting the tower of onion rings they see at our go-to restaurant, but of course they can't have them. I made these so we could enjoy amazing onion rings whenever we want.

Slice the onions into rings about ½ inch (1.3 cm) or so thick. Separate the rings and place on a plate.

In a bowl, combine the flour blend, breadcrumbs, salt, granulated garlic and black pepper. Stir to blend. Add the eggs and coconut milk and mix until creamy. Let the batter sit for 5 minutes to slightly thicken.

In a large skillet or Dutch oven, heat the coconut oil over medium heat. Bring the oil to 240°F (116°C) and maintain with a candy thermometer in the oil. Drop 4 or 5 onion rings into the batter and coat on all sides. Remove them from the batter with a fork and drop into the hot oil. Fry for about 4 minutes, then flip and fry them for 2 to 3 minutes on the second side. Using a spider strainer, remove them from the oil and place on a paper towel–lined plate. Continue until all the onion rings have been fried. If your batter gets too thick while it is sitting, add up to ¼ cup (60 ml) of coconut milk to it and stir to thin it out.

Prepare the campfire sauce: In a bowl, whisk together all the sauce ingredients.

MY TWO-CENTS

You can reheat the leftovers on a parchment paper–lined baking sheet in a 425°F (220°C) oven. Heat for about 6 minutes, or until they are crispy and they are ready to eat. You can also freeze these and reheat to serve. Simply let them thaw for 35 to 45 minutes and then place in a 425°F (220°C) oven to crisp for 12 to 14 minutes.

BACON-CHEDDAR POTATO SKINS

MAKES 12 POTATO SKINS

6 potatoes
½ cup (58 g) vegan cheddar cheese shreds
6 slices bacon, cooked and diced

RANCH DIPPING SAUCE
1 batch Simple From-Scratch Mayo (page 232)
1 tsp dried parsley
2 tsp (2 g) dried dill
1 tsp onion powder
1 tsp granulated garlic
¼ tsp sea salt
¼ tsp freshly ground black pepper
2 tsp (10 ml) fresh lemon juice
2 tbsp (30 ml) coconut milk, plus more if needed

3 green onions, diced, for garnish

Before I went gluten-free, potato skins were an appetizer that I always ordered. I loved the cheese with bacon on top of these delicious potatoes. The ranch sauce was essential as well. These are the perfect game-day recipe that is easy to make and that everyone will love.

Preheat the oven to 425°F (220°C). Line a baking sheet with parchment paper.

Wash the potatoes and pat them dry. Lay the potatoes on the prepared baking sheet and bake for 40 minutes.

Remove the potatoes from the oven. Once they are cool enough to handle, cut them in half lengthwise and place skin side down on the baking sheet. Spoon out a little bit of the center flesh so you have somewhere to add the toppings.

Reheat the oven to 425°F (220°C) if you turned it off while waiting for the potatoes to cool. Sprinkle the potatoes with the vegan cheddar cheese and bacon. Place back in the oven and bake for 6 minutes.

Prepare the sauce: In a small bowl, whisk together all the sauce ingredients. It will be thick as this is a dipping sauce. If you would like it more as a dressing, then add 2 additional tablespoons (30 ml) of coconut milk. The sauce may be stored in the fridge for up to 5 days.

Garnish the potatoes with the green onions and serve with the ranch dipping sauce.

MY TWO-CENTS
You can use regular dairy in place of the dairy-free options, if it does not need to be dairy-free.

You can make the potatoes a day ahead; just store them in the fridge after cooking. If you do this, you might want to leave them in the oven for an extra 5 minutes or so, to make sure they are heated through.

CAULIFLOWER WINGS

SERVES 4

VEGAN, PALEO &
WHOLE30 OPTION

2 heads cauliflower
2 tbsp (30 ml) avocado oil
¼ tsp sea salt

BUFFALO SAUCE

¼ cup (55 g) vegan butter, melted
1 tsp tapioca starch
½ cup (120 ml) hot sauce
1 tsp cider vinegar
1 tsp coconut aminos
1 tsp granulated garlic
½ tsp sea salt

Ranch Dipping Sauce (page 73)

Wings are a staple for game day. I never cared much for a traditional chicken wing, but I always loved cauliflower wings. In my opinion, these are a million times better than chicken wings—plus, these wings are vegan, and you can also make them Paleo/Whole30 if you wish. I have found myself making these every week since I created this recipe. They are full of spicy flavor and also healthy!

Preheat the oven to 425°F (220°C). Line a baking sheet with parchment paper.

Pull the cauliflower off the head into wing-size pieces. Place them in a colander and wash. Pat with a paper towel to dry and transfer them to a bowl. Drizzle them with the oil and sprinkle with the salt. Stir to coat all the cauliflower evenly. Lay the cauliflower in a single layer on the prepared baking sheet. Bake for 25 to 30 minutes, or until tender.

Meanwhile, prepare the buffalo sauce: In a medium-sized saucepan, melt the vegan butter over medium heat, then add the tapioca starch and whisk until dissolved. Remove from the heat and add the hot sauce, cider vinegar, coconut aminos, granulated garlic and salt. Stir until well blended. Set aside until the cauliflower is cooked.

Once the cauliflower is done, return the pieces to the bowl you used to coat them with oil. Pour the buffalo sauce on top and stir until all the pieces are completely coated with the sauce. Pour back onto the baking sheet and place back in the oven for 3 to 5 minutes, just to heat them up with the sauce.

Serve with the ranch dipping sauce.

MY TWO-CENTS
If you do not like spicy food, be aware that these have a kick. You can reduce the amount of hot sauce to ¼ cup (60 ml) and add ¼ cup (60 ml) of tomato sauce to make it less spicy.

BAGEL DOGS

SERVES 6

1 tbsp (12 g) active dry yeast

1 tbsp (13 g) sugar

1 cup (240 ml) warm water (110°F [43°C])

2 cups (320 g) + 2 tbsp (20 g) The Best Ever Gluten-Free All-Purpose Flour Blend (page 229), divided

1 tsp xanthan gum

½ tsp salt

1 tbsp (15 ml) avocado oil

6 hot dogs

Mustard or ketchup, for serving

My best friend's husband pestered me for years for a bagel dog recipe. She had put her family on a gluten-free diet, and he felt deprived. Because I knew bagels would be in this book, I decided to give him a bagel dog recipe, too. These are a fun gluten- and dairy-free spin on something a lot of us ate as kids. My kids had never had a bagel dog before I created this recipe, but now they love them.

Preheat the oven to 350°F (180°C). Line a baking sheet with parchment paper.

Activate the yeast: In a small bowl, add the yeast and sugar to the warm water and give it a stir. When it doubles in size, it is ready.

In a stand mixer fitted with the paddle attachment, combine 2 cups (320 g) of flour blend with the xanthan gum and salt. Blend on low speed for 30 seconds, then add the activated yeast and avocado oil while still mixing and blend for about 1 minute. Scrape the sides of the bowl and blend for 30 more seconds. Remove from the stand mixer and sprinkle 1 tablespoon (10 g) of the flour blend on the dough, then flip it and sprinkle with the other 1 tablespoon (10 g) of flour blend. Transfer to a sheet of parchment paper.

In a large stockpot, bring 4 quarts (3.8 L) of water to a boil. Pour some cold water into a bowl; you will use this to shape the bagel dogs. Cut the dough into 6 strips, using a knife dipped in the cold water. Wet your hands, grab 1 strip, place the hot dog in the middle and use your wet hands to shape the dough evenly around the hot dog. Repeat until all 6 are wrapped. Working in batches, place the bagel dogs in the boiling water and boil each batch for 4 minutes.

Once they are done boiling, transfer them to the prepared baking sheet. Bake for 40 minutes, flipping halfway through. Serve with your favorite mustard or ketchup.

MY TWO-CENTS

You can prepare the bagel dough (page 138) and use half of it to make these and the other half to make hot dog–free bagels (see page 138 for how to shape and boil/bake). These also taste amazing with the Everything Seasoning from my bagel recipe (page 138).

If avoiding dairy or corn, read hot dog labels carefully, as some brands include such additives.

BACON-WRAPPED BRUSSELS SPROUTS

SERVES 4

1 lb (455 g) Brussels sprouts, washed and trimmed
10 oz (280 g) bacon

RED WINE REDUCTION
2 cups (475 ml) red wine
⅓ cup (67 g) sugar
1 tsp vanilla extract
1 tsp ground cinnamon
¼ tsp ground nutmeg

These delicious Brussels sprouts have the perfect amount of sweet and savory flavor, and that is exactly how I want my appetizer. These are also the perfect snack to serve during a happy hour or cocktail party. The sweet red wine reduction is absolutely fabulous.

Preheat the oven to 425°F (220°C). Line a baking sheet with parchment paper.

Steam the Brussels sprouts for 8 minutes, then allow them to cool enough to handle.

Meanwhile, prepare the red wine reduction: In a medium-sized saucepan, combine all the reduction ingredients and give the mixture a good stir. Place over medium heat and bring to a light boil. Lower the heat slightly and simmer, stirring once a minute, for 30 minutes. Remove from the heat and let the sauce cool to thicken.

Wrap each Brussels sprout with a piece of bacon and secure the bacon with a toothpick. For some larger pieces, I used an entire slice of bacon, and for smaller pieces, I cut the bacon in half. Place on the prepared baking sheet. Bake the bacon-wrapped Brussels sprouts for 18 minutes, or until the bacon is crispy.

Serve the Brussels sprouts drizzled in the red wine reduction.

JALAPEÑO POPPER STUFFED MUSHROOMS

Jalapeño poppers and stuffed mushrooms have always been a favorite of mine. So, why not combine the two into the perfect appetizer? These taste just like a jalapeño popper, and the mushrooms have such a mild flavor that the jalapeño and cream cheese take center stage in this recipe. They have a nice kick and are addicting!

MAKES 12 TO 18 STUFFED MUSHROOMS

VEGAN

1 lb (455 g) whole baby bella mushrooms
1 tbsp (15 ml) avocado oil
3 tbsp (30 g) chopped garlic
⅓ cup (30 g) diced jalapeño peppers (I used jarred jalapeños)
1 (8-oz [225-g]) container vegan cream cheese
3 tbsp (21 g) gluten-free breadcrumbs

Preheat the oven to 425°F (220°C). Line a baking sheet with parchment paper.

Wash the mushrooms; remove and discard the stems.

Heat a large skillet over medium heat and add the avocado oil and garlic. Sauté for 2 to 3 minutes. Turn off the heat. Add the jalapeños and vegan cream cheese and stir until creamy and thoroughly mixed.

Spoon the cream cheese mixture into the mushrooms. Place the stuffed mushrooms on the prepared baking sheet. Sprinkle the breadcrumbs on top.

Bake for about 13 minutes, or until the tops are golden brown and the mushrooms are cooked through.

MY TWO-CENTS
If you don't like spiciness or you will be sharing these with kids, you can replace the jalapeños with mild green chiles.

COCONUT PRAWNS

We used to frequent our favorite seafood restaurant, and the coconut shrimp was one of our favorites. My husband and I missed it terribly after going gluten-free. He had been asking me for years to make him some, and I am glad I did. This is the perfect dish to serve as an appetizer, or even as a main course along with a salad, if you are munching while watching the game.

¾ cup (120 g) The Best Ever Gluten-Free All-Purpose Flour Blend (page 229)

3 large eggs, beaten

¾ cup (101 g) macadamia nuts

¾ cup (64 g) shredded coconut

3 tbsp (21 g) coconut flour

3 tbsp (24 g) tapioca starch

1 cup (225 g) coconut oil

1 lb (455 g) prawns, peeled, deveined and rinsed

PINEAPPLE DIPPING SAUCE

1 (20-oz [567-g]) can pineapple, drained

⅓ cup (80 ml) coconut milk

1 cup (85 g) shredded coconut

Line up 3 shallow dishes or pie dishes. Place the flour blend in the first dish and the eggs in the second dish. In a food processor, combine the macadamia nuts and coconut and process on high for 25 to 30 seconds, then pour the mixture into the third dish along with the coconut flour and tapioca starch. Stir to combine.

In a large skillet, heat the coconut oil over medium heat. While the oil is heating, coat the prawns. Add the prawns to the flour blend and coat on all sides; then add to the eggs, coating on all sides; and last, add to the macadamia mixture, coating on all sides.

Put the coated prawns in two batches of 5 to 6 prawns into the hot oil and cook for 4 to 5 minutes per side, or until crispy and golden brown. Once they are done, transfer them to a paper towel–lined plate to absorb the excess oil.

You can make the pineapple dipping sauce ahead or once the prawns are done: In a blender, combine all the sauce ingredients and blend on medium speed for 35 to 40 seconds, or until mixed together well. It will be a little thick because of the pineapple.

MY TWO-CENTS
The coating in this recipe is the same as the Macadamia Coconut-Crusted Mahi-Mahi (page 67). Double the coating and make both recipes at the same time for the perfect seafood appetizer and dinner.

FRIED ZUCCHINI

MAKES 32 PIECES

Fried zucchini is something that is impossible to find gluten-free. I was able to make this gluten-free by switching out the flour for my own flour blend (page 229) and using gluten-free breadcrumbs in place of regular breadcrumbs. I chose to fry the zucchini in avocado oil because it's a superclean oil that does well at high heat. This appetizer feels guilty, yet there is no guilt to be had here!

2 large eggs
¾ cup (120 g) The Best Ever Gluten-Free All-Purpose Flour Blend (page 229)
¾ cup (83 g) gluten-free panko-style breadcrumbs
1 tsp sea salt
¼ tsp freshly ground black pepper
2 tsp (6 g) granulated garlic
2 tsp (5 g) dried parsley
2 tsp (3 g) dried basil
1 cup (240 ml) avocado oil
4 medium-size zucchini, sliced in half lengthwise, then quartered
Ranch Dipping Sauce (page 73), for serving

In a shallow bowl or pie dish, beat the eggs. In a separate shallow pan or pie dish, combine the flour blend, breadcrumbs, salt, pepper, granulated garlic, parsley and basil. Mix until well blended.

In a large skillet, heat the avocado oil over medium heat.

As the oil heats, dip the zucchini sticks in the eggs and coat on all sides, then roll in the breadcrumb mixture to coat on all sides.

Working in batches, place the breaded zucchini in the hot oil. Cook for 2 to 3 minutes per side, or until the outside is golden brown and the zucchini is tender.

Serve with the ranch dipping sauce.

MY TWO-CENTS
If you can't find panko-style breadcrumbs, any gluten-free breadcrumbs will work.

CURRIED HUMMUS

MAKES 1 CUP
(245 G) HUMMUS

VEGAN

1 (15-oz [425-g]) can chickpeas,
drained and rinsed
Juice of ½ lemon
1 clove garlic
3 tbsp (45 g) tahini
⅓ cup (80 ml) olive oil
1½ tsp (3 g) curry powder
½ tsp sea salt

Hummus is such a simple recipe to make and you can make it with many different flavors. This one has a fun curry kick. Dip with your favorite gluten-free crackers or fresh vegetables. When we have a picnic or I have my friends over for lunch, hummus is a go-to of mine because it is so easy and fresh.

In a food processor or high-speed blender, combine all the ingredients and blend on high speed until smooth and creamy.

MY TWO-CENTS
If you do not like curry, simply omit it and add a few extra garlic cloves; you will have a traditional garlic hummus. You can use roasted garlic as well, to make it less spicy.

Savory Side Shows

A good side dish is almost as important as the main dish. This chapter is full of healthy and flavorful side dishes that my family loves and eats on a regular basis. You will find sides that go perfectly with your meats, such as the Orange-Maple Carrots (page 126) and Lemon-Pepper Asparagus (page 106). There are also side dishes that you will want to serve for holidays, such as the Scalloped Potatoes (page 93), Stuffed Acorn Squash (page 113) and Roasted Root Vegetables (page 98). Then, for summer barbecues, you will love the Brown Sugar and Bacon Baked Beans (page 114), Marinated Grilled Veggies (page 110), Homestyle Potato Salad (page 125), Summer Shrimp Mango Salad (page 121) and Pear and Prosciutto Arugula Salad (page 122).

BALLPARK GARLIC FRIES

SERVES 6

VEGAN, PALEO &
WHOLE30

7 medium-sized potatoes,
washed
1½ cups (337 g) coconut oil, for
frying
2 tbsp (30 ml) avocado oil
¼ cup (40 g) chopped garlic
1 tsp minced fresh parsley

When we used to go to ball games or concerts, the garlic fries were my go-to. I had to have them and loved them so much! Now, they are not safe due to cross-contamination, and every time I attend an event, the smell gets me. These are my way of enjoying one of my favorites again.

You will need to prep these one day ahead for best results, or at least in the morning if you are serving them that evening. Fill a large bowl with cold water and 1 cup (140 g) of ice cubes. Peel the potatoes and slice them into French fries, placing the potato slices into the ice water immediately after slicing. Refrigerate them overnight or until ready to cook.

When you are ready to cook them, in a large skillet or Dutch oven, heat the coconut oil over medium heat; a good temperature is around 250°F (120°C). You will have to make these in three batches. Take about one-third of the fries out of the water, transfer to a clean towel and blot to dry them off. Put the potatoes into the oil, cook for 15 minutes, then flip them and cook for 5 more minutes. If they are getting brown too fast, lower the heat.

Place the cooked fries on a paper towel–lined plate and fry the remaining potatoes. The fries will not be incredibly crispy by frying once. The key to crispy fries is to double fry them. Once you have fried all the potatoes, refry them again in batches for an additional 10 to 15 minutes per batch.

Toss the cooked fries with the avocado oil, garlic and parsley and serve immediately.

MY TWO-CENTS
You can use any oil in place of the coconut oil. Avocado oil would be my second choice.

These are best served right away. If they sit for a long time and start to become soft, place them in a 350°F (180°C) oven for a few minutes to allow them to crisp up again.

An easy hack is to prepare frozen french fries and then coat them with the avocado oil, garlic and parsley, if you want them in a pinch.

SCALLOPED POTATOES

SERVES 6

VEGAN

My entire life, I've loved scalloped potatoes. Most often, I had them out of the box, but on special holidays, my aunt would make them from scratch. After going dairy-free, I had to get creative on how to make these creamy and tender without compromising any flavor. To do this, I used tapioca starch to thicken and then nutritional yeast to get that thick and cheesy flavor. I chose coconut milk in place of dairy cream and then added seasonings. These are so delicious!

½ cup (120 ml) vegetable or chicken broth

2½ cups (590 ml) coconut milk

2 tbsp (16 g) tapioca starch

½ cup (64 g) nutritional yeast

1½ tsp (9 g) sea salt

1½ tsp (5 g) granulated garlic

¼ tsp freshly ground black pepper

¼ tsp paprika

Nonstick spray

6 medium-sized russet potatoes, sliced thinly

½ tsp dried parsley

Preheat the oven to 350°F (180°C).

In a medium-sized saucepan over medium heat, combine the broth, coconut milk, tapioca starch, nutritional yeast, salt, granulated garlic, pepper and paprika. Cook, stirring constantly, for 8 minutes. Lower the heat to medium-low and cook for an additional 6 minutes. Remove from the heat.

Coat a 2-quart (1.9-L) baking dish with nonstick spray. Then, layer in half of the potato slices, half of the sauce, then the remaining potato slices, and finally, the remainder of the sauce. Sprinkle the parsley on top and bake, uncovered, for 50 to 55 minutes, or until the potatoes are tender.

MY TWO-CENTS
You can always add some sliced ham to this if you don't need it to be vegan and want to take the flavor up a level.

RANCH POTATOES

SERVES 6

VEGAN, PALEO,
WHOLE30

3 lb (1.4 kg) red potatoes, washed and cut into bite-size cubes
¼ cup (60 ml) avocado oil
1 tsp dried parsley
2 tsp (2 g) dried dill
1 tsp onion powder
1 tsp granulated garlic
1 tsp sea salt
¼ tsp freshly ground black pepper

These easy oven-roasted potatoes taste amazing and are incredibly easy to make. All the seasonings blend together perfectly to give you a light ranch flavor. These serve six, so for my family, there are always some leftovers. I love reheating them the next day and having them with my breakfast. They are naturally Paleo/Whole30 and go great with any protein.

Preheat the oven to 425°F (220°C). Line a baking sheet with parchment paper.

Put the cubed potatoes in a bowl, drizzle with the avocado oil and stir to coat thoroughly.

In a separate small bowl, combine all the seasonings and stir to blend. Sprinkle the potatoes with half of the seasoning and stir, then add the remaining seasoning and stir until all the potatoes are coated well.

Place the potatoes in a single layer on the prepared baking sheet and bake for 45 minutes, or until tender on the inside and lightly crisp on the outside.

GARLIC MASHED POTATOES

SERVES 5

VEGAN &
WHOLE30 OPTION

2 heads garlic
1 tbsp (15 ml) avocado oil
6 cups (900 g) chopped russet potatoes
6 cups (1.4 L) water
¼ cup (55 g) vegan butter or ghee
½ cup (120 ml) coconut milk
½ tsp sea salt
¼ tsp freshly ground black pepper
¼ tsp granulated garlic

Mashed potatoes are a crowd-pleaser in my home and I make them often. I was tired of the traditional mashed potatoes, so I decided to liven them up with some fresh roasted garlic. The flavors are fantastic and we enjoy this on a regular basis. I truly enjoy the flavor the garlic brings to this dish.

Preheat the oven to 400°F (200°C).

Cut ¼ inch (6 mm) off the top of the garlic heads and peel the excess skin away. Place the heads on an 8-inch (20-cm) square piece of foil. Drizzle the oil on top and wrap the foil to cover the garlic. You will have a ball of foil-wrapped garlic.

Put the wrapped garlic on a baking sheet and bake for 40 minutes. Remove from the oven and open the foil to allow the garlic to cool, then pop out the roasted garlic from its skins (you will likely need to wait 20 minutes after opening the foil).

In a large pot, combine the potatoes with the water and bring to a boil. Allow the potatoes to cook until tender, about 20 minutes. Drain in a colander.

Place the potatoes in a stand mixer bowl or large bowl and add the whole roasted garlic, vegan butter, coconut milk, salt, pepper and granulated garlic. Using a stand mixer fitted with the paddle attachment or a hand mixer, mix on medium-low speed for 1 to 2 minutes, or until the potatoes are creamy to your liking.

MY TWO-CENTS
You can use any milk in place of the coconut milk, even dairy milk if this does not need to be nondairy. Cashew milk works well, but make sure it is unsweetened.

To make this Whole30, use ghee instead of vegan butter.

ROASTED ROOT VEGETABLES

These healthy vegetables can be prepped ahead of time for easy reheating when you need them. Each root vegetable has a unique and distinct flavor. You will get sweetness from the carrots, yam and sweet potato, but the turnip and parsnips add a little kick. I seasoned them as I would potatoes, and it was perfect. Serve with any protein or with eggs for breakfast.

SERVES 4
VEGAN, PALEO & WHOLE30

1 onion, sliced
1 turnip, peeled and cubed
1 sweet potato, peeled and cubed
1 yam, peeled and cubed
2 parsnips, peeled and cubed
4 carrots, peeled and chopped
4 cloves garlic
¼ cup (60 ml) avocado oil
1 tsp sea salt
1 tsp granulated garlic
¼ tsp freshly ground black pepper
1 tsp dried parsley
½ tsp dried sage
1 tsp dried rosemary
½ tsp paprika
½ tsp ground turmeric

Preheat the oven to 425°F (220°C). Line a baking sheet with parchment paper.

In a large bowl, combine all the veggies and the garlic cloves. Drizzle with the avocado oil and sprinkle with salt, granulated garlic, pepper, parsley, sage, rosemary, paprika and turmeric. Toss to coat evenly. Spread evenly on the prepared baking sheet. Bake for 45 minutes, or until all the vegetables are tender.

MY TWO-CENTS
You can get super-creative with this recipe, or make it easy with just a single kind of root vegetable. Anything goes, so whichever you can find at your local store will work.

CURRIED VEGETABLES

SERVES 4

VEGAN, PALEO & WHOLE30 OPTION

1 cup (100 g) green beans
2 cups (182 g) broccoli florets
3 cups (450 g) peeled and cubed russet potatoes
¼ cup (60 ml) avocado oil
1 (15-oz [425-g]) can chickpeas
1 tsp sea salt
1 tsp granulated garlic
¼ tsp freshly ground black pepper
1½ tsp (3 g) curry powder
¼ tsp ground turmeric

When I lived in Washington, there was a little Indian restaurant in the mall. It had amazing channa masala and curried veggies. My daughter and I would go a few times a month for lunch, and it was a great little outing while my son was at school. I re-created this recipe to enjoy it once again, and it is so darn good. Curry has a rich flavor and if you enjoy it, then you will love this recipe. I particularly love this alongside the Turmeric Sage Fried Chicken (page 63).

In a steamer pot, steam the veggies for 20 minutes.

When they are done, in a large skillet, heat the avocado oil over medium heat. Transfer the steamed veggies and chickpeas to the skillet and sprinkle them with the salt, granulated garlic, pepper, curry and turmeric. Toss to mix and cook for 3 minutes. Flip the veggies and cook for another 2 minutes.

MY TWO-CENTS
This is a great "clean-out-the-fridge" dish, because truly anything goes. You can use as much of any vegetable as you would like.

To make this Paleo/Whole30 compliant, simply swap the chickpeas for a different vegetable; carrots are a great option.

ROSEMARY-SAGE MUSHROOMS

SERVES 4
VEGAN, PALEO & WHOLE30 OPTION

3 tbsp (42 g) vegan butter or ghee

2 tbsp (20 g) diced garlic

½ tsp dried sage

½ tsp dried rosemary

2 fresh sage leaves

1 sprig fresh rosemary

8 oz (225 g) sliced white mushrooms

½ tsp sea salt

¼ tsp freshly ground black pepper

This healthy side dish is full of so much fabulous flavor. The rosemary and sage work together to make a simple dish into something spectacular. This cooks fast, so if you are looking for a quick side dish, then this is perfect. Serve this with chicken, steak or any other protein. It would also be perfect on top of cauliflower rice as well.

In a large skillet, melt the vegan butter over medium heat, then infuse the vegan butter by adding the garlic, dried sage, dried rosemary, fresh sage and fresh rosemary and sautéing for 1 minute. Add the mushrooms and sprinkle with the salt and pepper. Sauté, stirring every 30 seconds, for 8 to 10 minutes, or until tender.

MY TWO-CENTS
If you use ghee for this dish, it is Paleo/Whole30.

BACON GREEN BEANS

SERVES 4

PALEO & WHOLE30 OPTION

5 slices bacon, diced
1 lb (455 g) green beans, washed and trimmed
1 cup (240 ml) chicken broth
½ tsp sea salt
¼ tsp freshly ground black pepper
½ tsp granulated garlic

My stepdad makes these green beans every holiday. One year at Thanksgiving, I watched him make them. I have been making them ever since for most special occasions. The bacon gives the green beans an amazing flavor. They are soft, tender and delicious. My family often looks forward to this dish being served. My kids even help me with it by trimming all the green beans with me in the kitchen.

In a Dutch oven, sauté the bacon over medium heat, stirring once a minute, for 4 to 5 minutes. Add the green beans, broth, salt, pepper and granulated garlic. Cook, uncovered, for 10 minutes, then lower the heat to low, cover and simmer, stirring occasionally, for 1 hour to 1 hour and 20 minutes, or until the green beans are very tender and most of the liquid is gone. Remove the lid and cook off the rest of the liquid; this takes about 4 minutes. Now it's ready to serve.

MY TWO-CENTS
To make this Paleo/Whole30, you will need to use a compliant bacon.

When I am making this for a large gathering, I will double or even triple the recipe.

LEMON–PEPPER ASPARAGUS

SERVES 4

VEGAN, PALEO &
WHOLE30

1 lb (455 g) asparagus, washed
and trimmed
2 tbsp (30 ml) avocado oil
Juice of ½ lemon
Sprinkle of sea salt
½ tsp freshly ground black
pepper

When asparagus is in season, I buy it several times a week. It tastes great no matter how you make it, and this simple recipe gives it a fabulous citrus kick with a little bit of spiciness from the pepper. I often serve this warm alongside meat, but you could eat the leftovers cold, too.

Preheat the oven to 425°F (220°C). Place the asparagus on a baking sheet. Drizzle the oil and lemon juice on top and move the asparagus around in the pan so that each stalk gets coated evenly. Sprinkle with the salt and pepper.

Bake for 10 minutes.

MY TWO-CENTS
You might need to decrease or increase the cook time depending upon the size of your asparagus. You do not want to overcook it. When a fork pierces the asparagus nice and easy, it is done.

SPANISH CAULIFLOWER RICE

I grew up eating Spanish rice every single week of my life. It is a staple that my grandma Olga still makes to this day. Needing to have a cleaner diet that doesn't include rice on a regular basis inspired me to make this Paleo/Whole30 version of her recipe and it's pretty close. I use this in my Breakfast Enchilada Casserole (page 172), and it is perfect for any type of recipe in which you might want a Spanish-style rice but don't want the carbs.

SERVES 4
VEGAN, PALEO & WHOLE30

2 tsp (10 ml) avocado oil
1 cup (160 g) diced onion
3 tbsp (30 g) minced fresh garlic
2½ cups (250 g) riced cauliflower
1 (14.5-oz [411-g]) can diced tomatoes
¾ tsp granulated garlic
¾ tsp sea salt
Sprinkle of freshly ground black pepper
½ tsp ground cumin
¼ tsp chili powder

In a large skillet, heat the avocado oil over medium heat. Add the onion and garlic and sauté for 3 minutes. Add the riced cauliflower, diced tomatoes and seasonings. Cover and cook for 5 minutes, stirring halfway through.

MY TWO-CENTS
I also love stuffing bell peppers with this rice.

Watch your cook time; this can be overcooked very easily, which will make it mushy.

MARINATED GRILLED VEGGIES

SERVES 6

VEGAN, PALEO & WHOLE30

1 red onion, sliced

3 medium-sized zucchini, washed and sliced

8 oz (225 g) whole mushrooms, washed

1 bell pepper, washed, seeded and cubed

MARINADE

Juice of 2 lemons

½ cup (120 ml) white wine vinegar

1 tbsp (15 ml) avocado oil

1 tsp sea salt

¼ tsp freshly ground black pepper

1 tsp granulated garlic

½ tsp onion powder

½ tsp dried sage

1 tsp dried parsley

This healthy veggie dish is so simple, yet scrumptious and full of flavor. The great thing about a side dish like this is there is no way to go wrong. Any vegetable will work and you can play around with the marinade ingredients to create your own favorite flavor. You can roast these in the oven if it is winter, but I love to grill them.

Soak six wooden or bamboo skewers in water for at least 20 minutes (no need to soak if using metal skewers). Then, make kebabs by sliding the veggies alternately onto the skewers.

Prepare the marinade: In a small bowl, whisk together all the marinade ingredients. If you have a dish large enough, place all the kebabs in the bowl and pour the marinade over them, cover with foil. If not, you can place the kebabs in a large ziplock bag (take care not to puncture it with the skewers), pour the marinade inside, seal, then lay the bag flat. Allow the veggies to marinate in the fridge for 4 to 6 hours or overnight.

Grill for 30 to 35 minutes or roast in a 425°F (220°C) oven for 35 minutes.

STUFFED ACORN SQUASH

SERVES 4

PALEO & WHOLE30 OPTION

2 (2-lb [905-g]) acorn squashes
4 tsp (20 ml) avocado oil
¼ tsp sea salt

FILLING

3 tbsp + 1 tsp (50 ml) avocado oil
5 cloves garlic, diced
½ onion, diced
½ bell pepper, seeded and diced
8 oz (225 g) ground pork sausage
½ tsp granulated garlic
½ tsp sea salt
¼ tsp freshly ground black pepper
¼ tsp dried sage
1 tsp fresh or dried rosemary

These beautiful acorn squashes are so fun. The ground pork gives it a nice rich flavor and the onion and garlic make it hearty. When you dig in, you eat the squash along with each bite of the meat mixture, a perfect combination of sweet and savory. I love making food beautiful on its own, and because you literally serve it in the squash, it's like having it in a pretty bowl that you can eat.

Preheat the oven to 400°F (200°C).

Slice the squash in half lengthwise and spoon out the seeds. Coat the inside of each squash half with 1 teaspoon of the avocado oil and a sprinkle of salt (I used ¼ teaspoon of salt to cover all the squash). Place, cut side up, on a baking sheet or in a pie dish. Bake for 35 minutes.

Meanwhile, make the filling: In a large skillet, heat the avocado oil and sauté the garlic, onion and bell pepper for 4 to 5 minutes. Add the ground pork sausage and brown. While the sausage is browning, sprinkle with the granulated garlic, salt, black pepper, sage and rosemary and mix well. Once the sausage is cooked through, 5 to 8 minutes, remove from the heat and wait for the squash to finish cooking.

Remove the pan from the oven, fill each squash half with the filling and bake for an additional 20 minutes.

MY TWO-CENTS
Feel free to use different meats or to add your own favorite veggies and seasonings, but I truly love the flavor the ground sausage provides.

You can use grass-fed beef in place of the sausage if you want to make it Paleo/Whole30.

BROWN SUGAR AND BACON BAKED BEANS

SERVES 4 TO 6

2 tbsp (30 ml) avocado oil
1 onion, diced
3 tbsp (30 g) minced garlic
5 slices bacon, cut into 1-inch (2.5-cm) squares
¼ cup (65 g) tomato paste
¼ cup (60 ml) ketchup
1 tbsp (15 ml) cider vinegar
½ cup (115 g) light brown sugar
¼ cup (85 g) molasses
3 tbsp (45 ml) pure maple syrup
1 tsp sea salt
¼ tsp freshly ground black pepper
3 (15.5-oz [439-g]) cans navy beans, drained and rinsed

Nothing beats some delicious beans to go with your summer grilling. During the winter months, this pairs perfectly with my Slow-Cooked "Fall Off the Bone" Ribs (page 19). I never liked canned baked beans, and I try to keep our ingredients as clean as possible. These beans do not compromise any flavor and they are made with good-for-you ingredients. The best part is how easy they are to make.

Preheat the oven to 350°F (180°C).

In a large skillet, heat the avocado oil over medium heat and add the onion and garlic. Sauté until the onion is translucent, then add the bacon. Cook the bacon for 5 to 6 minutes, then add the tomato paste, ketchup, cider vinegar, brown sugar, molasses, maple syrup, salt and pepper. Stir and blend well.

Slowly add the beans and cover the beans with the sauce. Turn off the heat and transfer the beans to a baking dish. Cover the baking dish with foil and bake for 60 minutes.

MY TWO-CENTS
You can also use Great Northern beans in place of the navy beans, but they require a longer cook time of an additional 25 to 35 minutes.

WARM SPINACH SALAD

SERVES 4

PALEO & WHOLE30
OPTION

2 slices bacon, cut into ½-inch
(1.3-cm) pieces
¼ cup (35 g) pine nuts
¼ cup (28 g) slivered almonds
5 oz (140 g) baby spinach
1 tbsp (15 ml) red wine vinegar
Pinch of salt
Pinch of freshly ground black
pepper

I created this simple salad recipe right after going gluten-free. I was in need of something quick that I could have for lunch. The bacon gives the salad all the oil it needs, along with a salty flavor. I love the toasted pine nuts and almonds for that rich nutty taste and crunch. Nothing beats loading up on your greens for a simple lunch or side dish, and this salad will not feel like eating vegetables.

Place a large skillet over medium heat. Add the bacon. Cook for 1 minute and stir. Cook another few minutes, until the bacon is almost fully cooked, then add the pine nuts and almonds. Cook for about 45 seconds more, stirring constantly. Once the nuts start to toast, about 45 seconds, turn off the heat. Allow the pan to cool for 3 minutes.

Add the baby spinach, red wine vinegar, salt and pepper. Toss until coated. Remove from the pan and serve immediately.

MY TWO-CENTS
If your pan is too hot, the spinach will wilt fast. If you want crunchy spinach, then let the pan cool for longer. I like it slightly softened, but not wilted, and that is what these directions will achieve.

To make this recipe Paleo/Whole30, use compliant bacon.

GRILLED CHICKEN HARVEST SALAD

SERVES 4
PALEO

3 tbsp (45 ml) avocado oil
1 lb (455 g) boneless, skinless chicken breast
1 tsp sea salt
¼ tsp freshly ground black pepper
1 tsp granulated garlic
½ tsp paprika
5 oz (140 g) spring mix salad
¼ cup (25 g) pecan halves
¼ cup (28 g) slivered almonds
¼ cup (30 g) dried cranberries
1 apple, cored and sliced
Zest of ½ orange (reserve other orange half for dressing)

ORANGE VINAIGRETTE DRESSING
¼ cup (60 ml) olive oil
3 tbsp (45 ml) white wine vinegar
2 tbsp (30 ml) fresh orange juice
¼ tsp sea salt
1 tbsp (15 ml) pure maple syrup
Zest of ½ orange

I always serve a harvest salad during the fall months. There is something incredibly comforting about it, yet it is healthy and full of fabulous flavors. This one has been my favorite that I have created so far, and I am convinced it is the orange zest and orange vinaigrette dressing. The last time I made this, I shared it with my husband, but it was hard not to keep it to myself.

Heat the avocado oil in a grill pan over medium heat. Season the chicken evenly with the salt, pepper, granulated garlic and paprika and add to the pan. Cook for 2 minutes and flip, then continue to cook and flip until cooked through, 10 to 14 minutes. The total time will depend on how thick your chicken is; you can always cut the breast in half to see whether it is cooked through. Once the chicken is done, remove it from the pan and let it cool slightly, then cut into small slices.

Meanwhile, build your salad by placing the spring mix in your salad bowl and then sprinkling with the pecans, almonds, cranberries, apple slices and orange zest.

Prepare the dressing: In a small bowl, whisk together all the dressing ingredients. Drizzle the salad with the dressing and serve with the chicken slices on top.

MY TWO-CENTS
You can always swap the nuts for your own favorites, as well as dried fruit. Dried cherries are fabulous in this recipe, too.

SUMMER SHRIMP MANGO SALAD

SERVES 4

PALEO

5 oz (140 g) spring mix salad

2 tbsp (5 g) minced fresh cilantro

1 lb (455 g) precooked shrimp, rinsed

1½ cups (246 g) peeled, pitted and diced mango

¼ cup (28 g) slivered almonds

8 oz (225 g) cherry tomatoes, sliced in half

2 avocados, peeled, pitted and cubed

DRESSING

Juice of 1 lemon

¼ cup (60 ml) olive oil

¼ tsp granulated garlic

¼ tsp sea salt

¼ cup (85 g) honey

1 tbsp (15 ml) white wine vinegar

During the summer months, nothing beats a refreshing salad to cool you down. I love having cold shrimp on a salad for protein, and the mango gives it the perfect sweetness to balance all the flavors. The cilantro and avocado help keep the flavors cool and fresh, and I decided on a traditional vinaigrette so that the salad wouldn't be overpowered with sweetness.

To build your salad, place the fresh spring mix in your salad bowl and sprinkle evenly with the cilantro, then place the shrimp, mango, almonds, cherry tomatoes and avocados evenly over the greens.

Prepare the dressing: In a small bowl, whisk together all the dressing ingredients. Drizzle over the salad right before serving.

MY TWO-CENTS
You can replace the almonds with your favorite nuts, or leave them out if you're looking for a nut-free recipe.

PEAR AND PROSCIUTTO ARUGULA SALAD

SERVES 6

PALEO

DRESSING
¼ cup (60 ml) avocado oil
¼ cup (60 ml) red wine vinegar
¼ cup (60 ml) pure maple syrup
¼ tsp sea salt
¼ tsp granulated garlic
¼ tsp ground ginger

5 oz (140 g) baby arugula
2 cups (300 g) cherry tomatoes
4 oz (115 g) sliced prosciutto
½ cup (50 g) walnuts
1 Bosc pear, cored and thinly sliced

This salad is better than any arugula salad I have ordered at a restaurant. The savory prosciutto goes perfectly with the sweetness of the maple-balsamic dressing and the crisp sweet pears. It's a very pretty salad to serve when you have guests over, but I make it for myself all the time because I love it so much.

Prepare the dressing: In a small bowl, whisk together all the dressing ingredients with a fork. The oil and vinegar will separate, so you will need to restir before pouring onto your salad.

In a salad bowl or on a serving platter, combine the baby arugula, cherry tomatoes, prosciutto, walnuts and pear slices. Toss to mix and then drizzle with the dressing.

MY TWO-CENTS
When choosing a pear for this salad, use one that is not overly ripe. A slight softness is okay, but you want it to be firm overall for slicing and texture.

HOMESTYLE POTATO SALAD

SERVES 6

3 lb (1.4 kg) russet potatoes, washed, peeled and cubed

1 tsp salt, divided

¼ cup (56 g) Simple From-Scratch Mayo (page 232)

2 tsp (10 ml) prepared yellow mustard

½ red onion, diced

2 tbsp (30 g) sweet relish

2 hard-boiled large eggs, sliced

Summer and potato salad go hand in hand. This recipe is a mix of my best friend's mom's potato salad and my grandma's. I love them both so much, so I took the two and blended it into the perfect potato salad.

In a saucepan, combine the potatoes with water to cover, add ½ teaspoon of the salt and bring to a boil. Once the water begins to boil, cook for 12 minutes, until tender but not mushy.

Meanwhile, in a small bowl, stir together the mayo, yellow mustard, red onion, sweet relish and remaining ½ teaspoon of salt.

Once the potatoes are cooked, drain and transfer them to a large bowl. Add the mayo mixture to the potatoes and stir to combine. Top with the sliced hard-boiled eggs. Serve warm, or chill in the refrigerator.

MY TWO-CENTS
You can never go wrong here. Have fun with this recipe and feel free to add bacon, green onions or olives.

ORANGE-MAPLE CARROTS

SERVES 4

VEGAN & PALEO

1 lb (455 g) carrots, peeled and washed
1 tbsp (15 ml) avocado oil
½ tsp sea salt
1 tbsp (15 ml) pure maple syrup
1 tsp orange zest

These sweet carrots are a healthy side dish for any occasion. They are full of flavor and could not be easier to throw together. I love serving these alongside a weeknight dinner or at holiday gatherings. The orange zest gives a sweet citrus flavor along with the maple syrup to make these the perfect sweet vegetable side dish.

Preheat the oven to 425°F (220°C). Line a baking sheet with parchment paper.

Coat the carrots with the avocado oil and salt. Place in a single layer on the prepared baking sheet and bake for 17 minutes. Remove from the oven, drizzle the carrots with the maple syrup and sprinkle the orange zest all over them. Place back in the oven to bake for 3 more minutes, then remove from the oven and serve.

MY TWO-CENTS
If you want a more savory dish, you can replace the orange zest and maple syrup with seasonings and herbs of your choice. Add them at the same time as the sea salt and bake for 20 minutes.

Fluffy and Soft Breads & Dough

Most often, when I ask people what they miss the most since going gluten-free, they respond with "bread." Having bread for sandwiches or dinner rolls was something we had missed terribly for years. Fluffy and soft gluten-free breads didn't exist for a long time, but they have come a long way. These recipes took a lot of work to perfect, but they were worth it. They are not difficult; in fact, they are incredibly simple. You will never have to miss bread again. Nothing beats a soft and squishy loaf of Bakery-Style French Bread (page 145) or a fresh loaf of Sliceable Sandwich Bread (page 130). I have shared every bread in this chapter with my gluten-eating family and they love them all. Don't forget to share!

SLICEABLE SANDWICH BREAD

MAKES 1 LOAF

½ tsp coconut oil, for pan

1 tbsp (13 g) sugar

2 tbsp (24 g) active dry yeast

1½ cups (355 ml) warm water (110°F [43°C])

3 large egg whites

2 tbsp (30 ml) cider vinegar

1 tsp Paleo Grain-Free Baking Powder (page 231)

1 tsp salt

¼ tsp freshly ground black pepper

1½ tsp (4 g) xanthan gum

3 cups (480 g) The Best Ever Gluten-Free All-Purpose Flour Blend (page 229)

3 tbsp (45 ml) avocado oil

This was the one recipe that my blog followers requested over and over again. I was worried at first because bread is difficult to get right! This took many tries and tweaks, but it was totally worth it. This is, hands down, the best bread I have eaten since going gluten-free. I use it for Incredible Eggs Benedict (page 180) and French Toast Casserole (page 179), but we are guilty of just slicing and eating it with butter.

Preheat the oven to 350°F (180°C). For the best loaf, you will need a 7 x 4–inch (18 x 10–cm) loaf pan that is 4 inches (10 cm) tall. Oil the pan with the coconut oil.

Activate the yeast: In a small bowl, add the sugar and yeast to the warm water and give it a stir. When it doubles in size, 6 to 10 minutes, it is ready.

Meanwhile, in a stand mixer fitted with the whisk attachment, beat the egg whites on high speed for 5 minutes. Turn off the mixer and change to the paddle attachment. With the mixer turned off, add the activated yeast, cider vinegar, baking powder, salt, pepper and xanthan gum, then mix on low speed for 30 seconds. Add the flour blend, 1 cup (160 g) at a time, and mix on low speed for 1 minute. Drizzle in the avocado oil with the mixer on low speed and mix for an additional minute.

Pour the dough into the prepared loaf pan. Cover and let rise in a warm spot for about 20 minutes, or until the dough is three-quarters full in the pan. Keep an eye on it—if the dough rises too high, it could overflow and flop while it bakes.

Place the pan on the bottom rack of the oven and bake for 55 minutes, or until you have a nice golden crust and a butter knife inserted into the center comes out clean. Remove from the oven and allow to cool in the pan for 30 minutes, then remove and slice (do not leave in the pan for longer than 30 minutes or it will stick).

MY TWO-CENTS
When I was doing the recipe creation for this, I kept failing because of the loaf pan I was using. Use a loaf pan that is the same size as in the directions for success.

PERFECT POPOVERS

MAKES 6
POPOVERS

Some call them Yorkshire pudding, but in the United States they are commonly known as popovers. Popovers are an eggy and dense bread, almost like a roll but they pop up in the middle while cooking. These are an absolute must for soaking up gravy from your roast or stew. Nothing beats serving these popovers along with Classic Sunday Pot Roast (page 27) on a chilly winter night.

3 large eggs
1 cup (160 g) The Best Ever Gluten-Free All-Purpose Flour Blend (page 229)
Pinch of salt
½ cup (120 ml) coconut milk
1 tbsp (15 ml) melted vegan butter or ghee

Preheat the oven to 425°F (220°C). Place the empty popover pan in the oven and allow it to heat up, about 5 minutes.

In a blender, combine the eggs, flour blend, salt and coconut milk. Blend for 45 seconds.

Remove the popover pan from the oven. Pour the melted butter evenly into each popover cavity, then pour the batter evenly into each cavity. Bake for 20 minutes. Do not open the oven until the 20 minutes are over! Remove from the oven and allow the popovers to rest for at least 15 minutes before trying to remove them from the pan.

MY TWO-CENTS
You can use regular butter and whole milk in this recipe, if the popovers don't need to be dairy-free.

I cannot stress enough that the popover pan must be hot to start, so don't skip that step; also how important it is to not open the oven before the 20 minutes are up, or else the popovers will deflate.

If you don't have a popover pan, you can use a muffin pan, but they will not pop as much.

TO-DIE-FOR DINNER ROLLS

MAKES 9 ROLLS

1 tbsp (13 g) sugar

2 tbsp (24 g) active dry yeast

1 cup (240 ml) warm water (110°F [43°C])

½ cup (120 ml) coconut milk

2 tbsp (42 g) honey

2 tbsp (30 ml) melted vegan butter, divided

1 large egg

1½ tsp (9 g) sea salt

1 tbsp (15 ml) cider vinegar

2 tsp (5 g) xanthan gum

1 tsp Paleo Grain-Free Baking Powder (page 231)

¼ tsp freshly ground black pepper

1 tsp granulated garlic

1 tsp dried parsley

3 cups (480 g) The Best Ever Gluten-Free All-Purpose Flour Blend (page 229)

½ tsp coconut oil, for pan

They are truly the easiest and most delicious gluten- and dairy-free dinner rolls. Enjoy them with soup or salad and pasta, or make sandwiches with them. Whenever I make these, the kids get superexcited that we get to have bread with dinner.

Activate the yeast: In a small bowl, add the sugar and yeast to the warm water. Give it a stir and once it has doubled in size, 6 to 10 minutes, it is ready.

Meanwhile, in a stand mixer fitted with the paddle attachment, combine the coconut milk, honey and 1 tablespoon (15 ml) of the melted vegan butter and blend for 30 seconds. Add the activated yeast and egg and blend for 1 minute. Add the salt, cider vinegar, xanthan gum, baking powder, pepper, granulated garlic, parsley and flour blend. Blend for 2 minutes, scraping the sides of the bowl halfway through.

Oil a pie dish with the coconut oil and use an ice-cream scoop to scoop the dough into the prepared pie dish, placing the dough balls right next to one another, circling the inside of the dish, and then adding the last one right in the middle. Brush the tops with the remaining tablespoon (15 ml) of melted vegan butter. Cover with a clean towel, place in a warm spot and allow to rise for 30 minutes. While the rolls rise, preheat the oven to 350°F (180°C),

Once the rolls have risen, bake for 25 minutes, or until golden brown and a toothpick inserted into each roll comes out clean. Remove from the oven and allow the rolls to cool for 15 to 20 minutes in the pan before cutting apart.

MY TWO-CENTS

To store the baked rolls in the freezer, I suggest wrapping them with plastic wrap and placing in a freezer bag. Defrost and then reheat them by wrapping in foil and placing in a 350°F (180°C) oven to serve.

EASY ROLL-OUT PIE DOUGH

MAKES 1
PIECRUST

VEGAN

2 cups (320 g) The Best Ever
Gluten-Free All-Purpose Flour
Blend (page 229)
½ cup (112 g) vegan butter
¼ cup (55 g) coconut oil
1 tsp xanthan gum
½ tsp salt
½ cup (120 ml) ice water

MY TWO-CENTS

You can store this in the fridge for up to 3 days.

I keep hearing over and over how so many people have not made gluten-free pie dough successfully, and that is why I created this recipe. The secret to a perfect transfer is the plastic wrap.

This pie dough is incredibly easy to make. You can shape it easily and the flaky, buttery flavor is perfect for your dessert, potpie and quiche recipes. Pie dough is intimidating for many, but I made this foolproof recipe so you can enjoy your favorite dishes again.

In a large bowl, combine the flour blend, vegan butter, coconut oil, xanthan gum and salt. Use a pastry cutter to press repeatedly into the mixture for about 1 minute, or until you have lots of little dough balls the size of peas.

Add the ice water and continue to press your pastry cutter into the mixture. Once the mixture starts to form into a large ball, scrape all the dough off the pastry cutter and begin to knead the dough with your hands. Knead until it is smooth and formed into a disk. Wrap the disk in plastic wrap and refrigerate for 1 hour.

Place plastic wrap on the surface you will be using to roll it out. I used two large sheets of plastic wrap.

Remove the pie dough from the fridge and place it on top of the plastic wrap; if it is really hard, allow it to soften for a few minutes before rolling out. Put two additional sheets of plastic wrap over the top of the dough, overlapping just in the middle. You want enough plastic wrap to be able to roll it out without pushing the dough over the edges (the plastic wrap is an important part of rolling your dough out successfully).

Once your dough is rolled out to your desired dimension, remove the top layer of plastic wrap. Take your hand and gently shimmy it under the plastic wrap that is under your dough, just gently lifting it from the countertop to make your transfer successful.

Lay your pie dish on top of the dough. In one quick motion, you need to flip it. Don't overthink this part—just go for it. Once it is flipped, you can cut off the excess dough and shape the edges. If some pieces fall off the edges, it is very easy to pinch extra dough into those spots to reshape it.

Once flipped, push the dough down into the pan and shape the edges however you desire. Fill with your favorite filling and bake according to the recipe instructions.

EVERYTHING–BUT-THE–GLUTEN BAGELS

MAKES 6 TO 9 BAGELS

VEGAN

EVERYTHING SEASONING
½ tsp sea salt
1 tsp poppy seeds
1 tsp granulated garlic
1 tsp onion powder
1½ tsp (4 g) white sesame seeds
1½ tsp (4 g) black sesame seeds

BAGEL DOUGH
2 tbsp (24 g) active dry yeast
2 tbsp (26 g) sugar
2 cups (475 ml) warm water (110°F [43°C])
4¼ cups (680 g) The Best Ever Gluten-Free All-Purpose Flour Blend (page 229)
2 tsp (5 g) xanthan gum
1 tsp salt
2 tbsp (30 ml) avocado oil

Soft, squishy and chewy bagels! These are the perfect bagels you have been craving and needing in your life. These are a total weakness of mine, and I love them all seasoned up and smothered in vegan cream cheese.

In a small bowl, combine all the everything seasoning ingredients and stir.

Prepare the bagel dough: Activate the yeast. In a separate small bowl, add the yeast and sugar to the warm water and give it a stir. When it doubles in size, 6 to 10 minutes, it is ready.

Preheat the oven to 350°F (180°C). Line a baking sheet with parchment paper. In a large stockpot, bring 4 quarts (3.8 L) of water to a boil.

In a stand mixer fitted with the paddle attachment, combine the flour blend, xanthan gum and salt. Blend on low speed for 30 seconds, then add the activated yeast and avocado oil while still mixing. Blend for about 1 minute. Scrape the sides of the bowl and blend for 30 more seconds. Remove the dough from the stand mixer and form it into 6 to 9 balls. Use your finger to puncture a hole in the middle of each ball and shape the bagels with wet hands, if needed.

Working in batches (I did it in 3), boil the bagels for 3 minutes. Place the boiled bagels on the prepared baking sheet and sprinkle the everything seasoning on top. Bake for 40 minutes, flipping halfway through. The bagels should be slightly firm and golden.

MY TWO-CENTS
You can use half of this recipe to make bagels and the other half to make Bagel Dogs (page 77).

BUTTERY BREAD-STICKS

SERVES 8

VEGAN

2 tbsp (24 g) active dry yeast

1 tbsp (13 g) sugar

1½ cups (355 ml) warm water (110°F [43°C]), divided

2½ cups (400 g) The Best Ever Gluten-Free All-Purpose Flour Blend (page 229)

1 tsp xanthan gum

½ tsp sea salt

½ tsp dried basil

½ tsp granulated garlic

2 tbsp (30 ml) avocado oil

½ cup (120 ml) marinara sauce, for dipping

TOPPING

2 tbsp (30 ml) melted vegan butter

½ tsp sea salt

¼ tsp granulated garlic

I miss the days of going to our local Italian restaurant and getting a side of breadsticks along with our pasta. Breadsticks are actually not too difficult to make. The dough is very similar to pizza crust, except you don't top it. I've been making these to curb our breadstick craving and they are delicious.

Activate the yeast: In a small bowl, add the yeast and sugar to 1 cup (240 ml) of the warm water and give it a stir. When it doubles in size, 6 to 10 minutes, it is ready.

Preheat the oven to 350°F (180°C). Line a baking sheet with parchment paper.

In a stand mixer fitted with the paddle attachment, combine the flour blend, xanthan gum, salt, basil and granulated garlic. Mix on low speed for 30 seconds. Add the activated yeast and blend for 1 minute. Add the avocado oil and remaining ½ cup (120 ml) of warm water and blend for another minute.

Divide the dough into 2 equal pieces and place both on the prepared baking sheet. Use a wet spatula or wet hands to shape each dough into a 9 x 6–inch (23 x 15–cm) rectangle, spacing them 2 inches (5 cm) apart. Let the dough rest in a warm place to rise for 15 minutes, then bake for 15 minutes, or until the outside is slightly golden and a toothpick inserted into a breadstick comes out clean.

Remove from the oven and brush it with the melted vegan butter, salt and granulated garlic. Slice into sticks and serve with your favorite marinara sauce.

MY TWO-CENTS
To freeze these, instead of baking for 15 minutes, bake for only 10 minutes, allow to cool, then freeze. To reheat, simply allow the semibaked dough to thaw and then bake for 8 to 10 minutes at 350°F (180°C). Brush with the topping.

A pizza cutter works perfectly to slice these into breadsticks.

RESTAURANT-STYLE CROUTONS

MAKES 5 CUPS (375 G) CROUTONS

5 cups (375 g) cubed Sliceable
Sandwich Bread (page 130)
¼ cup (60 ml) avocado oil
½ tsp sea salt
½ tsp granulated garlic
½ tsp dried basil
½ tsp dried parsley

Who misses ordering a salad when you go out with big, delicious, crispy croutons all over your salad? Me! I love making homemade croutons, because they are so simple, yet give a salad an extra layer that makes a huge difference. If you need a little comfort on top of your salad, these definitely do the trick.

Set the oven broiler to high. Line a baking sheet with parchment paper.

In a bowl, combine the cubed bread with the avocado oil, tossing the bread to coat all the pieces evenly with oil. Sprinkle the salt, granulated garlic, basil and parsley all over the bread and toss again to thoroughly mix the seasonings.

Evenly spread out the croutons on the prepared baking sheet and broil for 5 minutes on the middle rack in the oven, then flip them and broil for another 2 minutes. You need to keep a close eye on them—never walk away, and use the oven light to watch them the entire time to ensure they do not burn.

MY TWO-CENTS
Save the heels from loaves of bread in the freezer and use them to make the croutons when you have enough. This is the perfect recipe for repurposing stale bread, too.

BAKERY-STYLE FRENCH BREAD

MAKES 2 LOAVES

2 tbsp (24 g) active dry yeast
1 tbsp (13 g) sugar
1 cup (240 ml) warm water
(110°F [43°C])
3 large egg whites
2 tbsp (30 ml) cider vinegar
1 tsp sea salt
1 tsp xanthan gum
Pinch of freshly ground black
pepper
2¼ cups (360 g) The Best Ever
Gluten-Free All-Purpose Flour
Blend (page 229)
3 tbsp (45 ml) avocado oil

Nothing beats a freshly baked loaf of French bread. The smell fills the house and brings joy. This French bread is free of many allergens, yet it is still flavorful, moist and even squishy. Plus, no rising time! All of my family members who are not gluten-free love this bread.

Preheat the oven to 350°F (180°C). Line a 2-loaf baguette pan with parchment paper.

Activate the yeast: In a small bowl, add the yeast and sugar to the warm water and give it a stir. When it doubles in size, 6 to 10 minutes, it is ready.

In a stand mixer fitted with the paddle attachment, beat the egg whites on medium speed for 4 minutes. You should have a nice white foam on top. You need the foam to make the bread airy. Add the cider vinegar and activated yeast and mix on low speed until just blended in. Add the salt, xanthan gum, pepper and flour blend. Mix on medium-low speed until blended together, about 2 minutes, scraping the sides of the bowl with a spatula halfway through. Reduce the mixer speed to low and add the avocado oil; blend it into the dough.

Spoon the dough evenly into the prepared baguette pan. You can use a wet spatula to shape the bread, if needed, and to smooth out any rough edges. Make several slits on the diagonal along the tops of the baguette dough.

Bake for 55 minutes, or until the breads have a beautiful, light golden brown crust.

Remove from the oven and allow to cool for 15 minutes before handling the bread and cutting it open.

MY TWO-CENTS
A baguette or French bread pan is essential for this recipe.

Feel free to bake these ahead of time and to freeze them. To reheat, preheat the oven to 350°F (180°C). Simply remove the bread from the freezer and allow it to thaw, then wrap in foil and heat in the oven for 10 minutes.

TRADITIONAL FLOUR TORTILLAS

MAKES 8 MEDIUM-
SIZE TORTILLAS

VEGAN

I grew up enjoying homemade tortillas often, and I learned how to make them as a preteen. We always had the ingredients for tortillas, so I would make them often during summer vacation and have them for lunch with tuna or just butter. This is my aunt Cheryl's recipe, but adapted to be gluten-free. It needed a few tweaks—such as the gluten-free flour, the water-to-oil ratio and the guar gum—but they are legit. These are the best-tasting gluten-free tortillas I've ever had.

3 cups (480 g) The Best Ever Gluten-Free All-Purpose Flour Blend (page 229)

1½ tsp (3 g) guar gum or xanthan gum

1 tbsp (12 g) Paleo Grain-Free Baking Powder (page 231)

1½ tsp (9 g) sea salt

1 cup + 2 tbsp (270 ml) warm water (110°F [43°C])

¼ cup (60 ml) vegetable or canola oil

In a medium-sized bowl, combine the flour blend, guar gum, baking powder and salt and whisk well. Add half of the warm water and stir, then add the other half. Add the oil, then knead the dough with your hands. Cover the dough with a clean towel and let rest for 30 minutes.

At the 30-minute point, heat a cast-iron skillet over medium heat (cast iron is important to getting good texture in traditional tortillas).

To roll out the tortillas, put a piece of parchment paper or plastic wrap on the counter and grab a ball of dough about 2 inches (5 cm) in diameter. Place it in the middle of the paper and add another piece of paper on top, then roll out with a rolling pin. You want the rolled-out dough to be as flat as possible while still being able to peel it off the paper. If you want the edges perfect, use a knife to cut off the jagged edges. Repeat to shape the remaining tortillas.

Working one at a time, place a tortilla in the hot skillet and cook for about 30 seconds per side. It will start to bubble and darken in color. After each tortilla has been cooked, place them in a tortilla warmer to keep warm until you are ready to serve them.

MY TWO-CENTS

I typically only use avocado or coconut oil, but in this recipe I recommend either vegetable or canola oil; they help with the texture.

You can also freeze the raw tortillas. To do this, use plastic wrap underneath and on top of each tortilla, layer them on top of one another, then store them in a freezer bag large enough for them to stay flat. To heat, allow them to mostly thaw and then cook in a cast-iron skillet as directed.

Morning Glory

Breakfast is such an important meal, and it often gets overlooked. On the weekends, my daughter Claire and I love making a delicious breakfast for the family together. This chapter is full of glorious, beautiful breakfasts that you will love serving on Sunday mornings, for brunches and on special occasions. Here, you have savory dishes, such as the Fully Loaded Potato-Crusted Quiche (page 153); comfort food, such as the From-Scratch Biscuits and Gravy (page 171); as well as scones (pages 158 and 161), traditional muffins (pages 154 and 157), Cherry Hand Pies (page 162), sticky buns (page 165) and crepes (page 150).

SUNDAY MORNING STRAWBERRY CREPES

MAKES
7 CREPES

4 large eggs

1½ cups (355 ml) coconut milk

2 cups (320 g) The Best Ever Gluten-Free All-Purpose Flour Blend (page 229)

1 tsp vanilla extract

2 tbsp (30 ml) maple syrup

Pinch of salt

¼ cup (60 ml) melted coconut oil

Nonstick spray

FILLING

1 (17-oz [482-g]) jar strawberry preserves

7 tbsp (105 ml) Coconut Whipped Cream (page 221)

2 cups (340 g) washed, hulled and sliced strawberries

1 tbsp (8 g) Grain-Free Powdered Sugar (page 230), for dusting

Crepes are an absolute treat and incredibly easy to make. I have been making this crepe recipe often because it was such a hit with all of my non-gluten-free friends that they have been requesting them. Crepes can be made savory or sweet and can be enjoyed any time of day. This is one of my go-to recipes for brunches and gatherings.

In a blender, combine the eggs, coconut milk, flour blend, vanilla, maple syrup and salt and blend for 1 to 2 minutes, or until a thin batter forms. Drizzle in the melted coconut oil and blend for another 30 seconds.

Heat a shallow, medium-sized skillet over medium heat. Spray the pan with nonstick spray and pour a thin layer of batter (about ¼ cup [60 ml]) into the pan, tilting the pan from side to side to fill the pan with the batter. Allow it to cook for 2 minutes per side. Transfer to a plate and continue until all the crepes are made.

Fill each crepe with 1 tablespoon (20 g) of preserves, 1 tablespoon (15 ml) of coconut whipped cream and sliced strawberries. Dust with powdered sugar and serve.

MY TWO-CENTS
Feel free to buy premade coconut whipped cream to make this recipe faster.

FULLY LOADED POTATO-CRUSTED QUICHE

SERVES 4

PALEO & WHOLE30 OPTION

Nonstick spray
3 slices bacon, diced
½ bell pepper, seeded and diced
½ onion, diced
1 cup (70 g) mushrooms, diced
2 cups (60 g) baby spinach
2 potatoes, sliced into thin rounds (I used a mandoline)
5 large eggs
¾ cup (175 ml) coconut milk
½ tsp sea salt
Pinch of freshly ground black pepper

Quiche is one of my favorite comfort foods. I grew up with my aunt Cheryl making quiche from time to time, and it was always something I looked forward to. I started making quiche as an adult in my early 20s, but when I became gluten- and dairy-free, it was time to experiment and find new ingredients that still tasted great to use in a quiche. I found that coconut milk and vegan cheese worked very well along with the same ingredients that I was using before. For this recipe, I used slices of potatoes to keep it super-healthy and simple. It's honestly faster to use potatoes than to make a piecrust. This Paleo recipe is perfect for breakfast, lunch or dinner.

Preheat the oven to 425°F (220°C). Spray a pie dish with nonstick spray.

In a large skillet, sauté the bacon. Once the bacon has started to release some of its fat, add the bell pepper, onion, mushrooms and baby spinach. Sauté for 7 to 10 minutes.

Line the prepared pie dish evenly with the potato slices. Pour the sautéed mixture over the potatoes. In a medium-sized bowl, whisk together the eggs, coconut milk, salt and black pepper until frothy, then pour the egg mixture on top of the veggies.

Cover with foil and bake for about 50 minutes; a butter knife inserted into the center should come out clean.

MY TWO-CENTS

You can use any veggies you have on hand in this recipe.

You can use the Easy Roll-Out Pie Dough (page 137), if you want a traditional quiche.

To make this recipe Paleo/Whole30, use compliant bacon and coconut milk.

BLUEBERRY COFFEE CAKE MUFFINS

MAKES 24 MUFFINS

2 large eggs

1 cup (200 g) granulated sugar

2 tsp (10 ml) vanilla extract

½ cup (120 ml) coconut milk

1½ cups (368 g) applesauce

¾ cup (175 ml) melted coconut oil

1 tsp ground cinnamon

½ tsp ground nutmeg

1 tsp Paleo Grain-Free Baking Powder (page 231)

1 tsp baking soda

1½ tsp (4 g) xanthan gum

¼ tsp salt

2 cups (320 g) The Best Ever Gluten-Free All-Purpose Flour Blend (page 229)

2 cups (290 g) blueberries

CRUMB TOPPING

¼ cup (55 g) vegan butter

⅓ cup (53 g) The Best Ever Gluten-Free All-Purpose Flour Blend (page 229)

½ cup (115 g) light brown sugar

1 tsp ground cinnamon

¼ cup (28 g) chopped pecans

I created this recipe for my best friend who missed the blueberry coffee cake from her old coffee shop. I had never tried blueberries in coffee cake before, and boy, was I missing out! The sweetness of the blueberries and the crumb topping make this the perfect brunch recipe.

Preheat the oven to 350°F (180°C). Line 24 wells of a muffin pan or pans.

In a stand mixer fitted with the paddle attachment, beat together the eggs, granulated sugar, vanilla and coconut milk for 1 minute on low speed. Add the applesauce, melted coconut oil, cinnamon and nutmeg. Mix for 2 minutes on low speed, then turn off the mixer.

Add the baking powder, baking soda, xanthan gum, salt and flour blend. With the mixer on low speed, beat until all the dry ingredients are mixed into the batter, then increase the speed to medium. Mix for 3 minutes, scraping the sides of the bowl halfway through. Fold in the blueberries.

Prepare the crumb topping: In a medium-sized bowl, combine all the topping ingredients. Mix with a fork until you have a crumb mixture.

Spoon ¼ cup (60 ml) of batter into each prepared muffin well. Place 1½ teaspoons (about 6 g) of the crumb topping on top of each muffin. Bake for 17 minutes, or until a toothpick inserted into the center of a muffin comes out clean.

Remove the muffins from the oven and let them cool in the pan for 15 to 20 minutes. The butter from the crumb will melt onto the bottom of the muffin cavities and liners. Remove the muffins from the pan and place on a wire rack (I lined my rack with paper towels to soak up the excess butter). Allow them to cool for another 20 minutes before serving.

MY TWO-CENTS
You could omit the blueberries altogether or use a different fruit, if desired.

APPLE-CINNAMON MUFFINS

Apple-cinnamon muffins are fabulous during the fall months, but can be enjoyed all year long. When I have lots of extra apples during apple season, this recipe is one of my go-tos to make and share with my friends and family. They are perfect for bringing over to a friend's house for coffee or sharing with your children's school staff. These muffins are sure to bring a smile to the face of anyone you decide to share them with.

1 cup (230 g) vegan vanilla yogurt
½ cup (125 g) applesauce
½ cup (112 g) vegan butter, at room temperature
2 large eggs
2 tsp (10 ml) vanilla extract
1 cup (225 g) light brown sugar
Pinch of salt
2 tsp (8 g) Paleo Grain-Free Baking Powder (page 231)
1½ tsp (3 g) ground cinnamon
¼ tsp ground nutmeg
1 tsp xanthan gum
2 cups (320 g) The Best Ever Gluten-Free All-Purpose Flour Blend (page 229)
1 apple, peeled, cored and diced

Preheat the oven to 350°F (180°C). Line 12 wells of a muffin pan.

In a stand mixer fitted with the paddle attachment, combine the vegan vanilla yogurt, applesauce, vegan butter, eggs, vanilla and brown sugar. Mix on medium speed for 3 minutes, or until well blended.

Add the salt, baking powder, cinnamon, nutmeg, xanthan gum and flour blend. Mix on medium speed for 3 minutes, scraping the sides of the bowl halfway through. Fold in the apples and blend for about 1 minute, or until they are blended throughout the batter.

Scoop the batter evenly into the prepared muffin wells; I used an ice-cream scoop for this. Bake for 28 minutes, or until a toothpick inserted into the center of a muffin comes out clean.

Remove from the oven and allow the muffins to cool in the pan for about 15 minutes before handling.

MY TWO-CENTS
Any apple will work for this recipe, but I prefer sweeter apples over tart ones. I used gala when I created this recipe.

CHOCOLATE-CHERRY SCONES

MAKES 9 SCONES

VEGAN

I love a good high tea, and scones are an important part of any tea party. These chocolate-cherry scones are fun because of the tart cherry and sweet, decadent chocolate chips. The two flavors balance each other well and are perfect in a crumbly delicious scone. The last time I made these, they were on the counter and my family began to help themselves—I blinked and they were gone.

2¼ cups (360 g) The Best Ever Gluten-Free All-Purpose Flour Blend (page 229)
2 tsp (8 g) Paleo Grain-Free Baking Powder (page 231)
½ tsp baking soda
Pinch of salt
¼ cup (55 g) firm coconut oil
¼ cup (60 ml) pure maple syrup
1 tbsp (15 ml) cider vinegar
¾ cup (175 ml) light coconut milk
½ cup (88 g) vegan chocolate chips
½ cup (60 g) dried cherries

GLAZE
½ cup (60 g) Grain-Free Powdered Sugar (page 230)
1 tsp coconut milk

Preheat the oven to 350°F (180°C). Line a baking sheet with parchment paper.

In a bowl, combine the flour blend, baking powder, baking soda and salt. Whisk until well combined. Add the firm coconut oil and cut it in with a pastry blender until small balls begin to form. Add the maple syrup, cider vinegar and coconut milk and blend until the liquids are absorbed. Add the chocolate chips and dried cherries and stir or knead the mixture until they are evenly distributed.

Scoop the mixture onto the prepared baking sheet, using an ice-cream scoop, to form 9 scones. Press the scones down and shape them a little with your hands, if needed. Bake for 20 minutes, or until a toothpick inserted into the center of a scone comes out clean.

Remove from the oven and allow them to cool on the baking sheet.

Meanwhile, prepare the glaze: In a small bowl, stir together the powdered sugar and coconut milk. Drizzle on top of the scones and serve.

MY TWO-CENTS
You can use any dried fruit in this recipe in place of the cherries, if you desire.

VANILLA BEAN SCONES

Scones are a traditional British recipe that usually resembles a biscuit, but they are a little sweeter. Often, for a tea party, a plain scone is served with clotted cream and lemon curd. I enjoy that, but I wanted to create a scone recipe with a fun twist. The light hint of vanilla bean with the icing drizzle makes this crumbly scone a wonderful treat. It is not overwhelmingly sweet, but the perfect amount of glaze makes it truly enjoyable. This is a great afternoon pick-me-up with a cup of tea.

MAKES 8 SCONES

VEGAN

2¼ cups (360 g) The Best Ever Gluten-Free All-Purpose Flour Blend (page 229)
2 tsp (8 g) Paleo Grain-Free Baking Powder (page 231)
½ tsp baking soda
Pinch of salt
2 tbsp (26 g) granulated sugar
¼ cup (55 g) firm coconut oil
¼ cup (60 ml) maple syrup
1 tbsp (15 ml) cider vinegar
1 tbsp (15 ml) vanilla extract
1 vanilla bean, scraped
¾ cup (175 ml) light coconut milk

GLAZE

½ cup (60 g) Grain-Free Powdered Sugar (page 230)
1 vanilla bean, scraped
1 tsp vanilla extract
2½ tsp (13 ml) coconut milk

Preheat the oven to 350°F (180°C). Line a baking sheet with parchment paper.

In a bowl whisk together the flour blend, baking powder, baking soda, salt and granulated sugar. Add the firm coconut oil and cut in with a pastry cutter until small balls form. Don't overdo it; it takes about 30 seconds. Add the maple syrup, cider vinegar, vanilla extract, scraped vanilla bean and coconut milk and blend until all the liquids are absorbed and the dough is well blended; you can knead with your hands, too.

Scoop the mixture onto the prepared baking sheet, using an ice-cream scoop, to form 8 scones. You can also use wet hands to shape them, if needed. Bake for 20 minutes.

Meanwhile, prepare the glaze: In a small bowl, combine the powdered sugar, scraped vanilla bean, vanilla extract and coconut milk and whisk until smooth.

Remove the scones from the oven and allow them to cool completely on the pan, then drizzle the glaze over the top. These taste best when eaten the same day they are made.

MY TWO-CENTS
These scones are very versatile. You can add any mix-ins to the batter.

CHERRY HAND PIES

MAKES 9 HAND PIES

VEGAN

1 batch Easy Roll-Out Pie Dough (page 137)
9 tbsp (180 g) cherry preserves

ICING

1½ cups (180 g) Grain-Free Powdered Sugar (page 230)
Pink food coloring (optional)
2 tbsp (30 ml) coconut milk

Sprinkles (optional)

With our multiple food allergies, my kids had never had a Pop-Tart until I created this recipe. I grew up loving and enjoying them, so it was special to me when I made this for them to have. I equally enjoy them, often overindulging when I make them. The best part is that these are made with better ingredients than the commercial kind you could purchase at the store.

Preheat the oven to 350°F (180°C). Line a baking sheet with parchment paper.

Roll out the pie dough, using plastic wrap, to be about ¼ inch (6 mm) thick. Cut the dough into 3 x 4–inch (7.5 x 10–cm) rectangles (I used a straight edge and pizza cutter). Remove the excess dough around the rectangles. I had to roll out the dough in two batches to make the 18 rectangles needed.

Place 1 tablespoon (20 g) of the preserves in the center of a rectangle, and then place another dough rectangle on top. Use a fork to press the edges together to give it the Pop-Tart look.

Place the hand pies on the prepared baking sheet and bake for 25 minutes, or until the crust is golden brown and the filling is bubbling. Some of the preserves might melt out during baking, but that's okay.

Remove from the oven and allow to cool on the pan for 10 minutes, then transfer to a wire rack and allow to cool for about 20 minutes.

Prepare the icing: In a small bowl, stir together the powdered sugar, pink food coloring (if using) and coconut milk. Drizzle or pour onto the top of the cooled hand pies and add sprinkles, if desired. Allow the icing to set for about 20 minutes, then serve.

MY TWO-CENTS
If the dough cracks while you are transferring the rectangles to cover the preserves, you can pinch off a piece of leftover dough and use it as a patch. Don't worry about the tops looking perfect, because you can cover it with icing, if needed.

If you are avoiding corn and/or dairy, make sure to check the ingredients of the sprinkles.

PECAN STICKY BUNS

Finding a gluten-free sticky bun that is also dairy-free has been an impossible task since going gluten-free. I don't know about you, but every time I go to the mall, the sensational smell of cinnamon buns fills my senses. That is why I created this sticky bun recipe. These are gooey and full of pecan goodness. I have been told that these are the real deal by friends who are not gluten-free, and I have to agree. These will absolutely hit the spot and are well worth the work!

MAKES 8 TO 10 BUNS

1 tbsp (13 g) sugar

2½ tsp (10 g) active dry yeast

1½ cups (355 ml) warm coconut milk (110°F [43°C])

3 cups (480 g) The Best Ever Gluten-Free All-Purpose Flour Blend (page 229)

1 cup (128 g) tapioca starch

½ tsp salt

2 tsp (5 g) xanthan gum

1 tbsp (12 g) Paleo Grain-Free Baking Powder (page 231)

2 large eggs, separated

¼ cup (55 g) vegan butter, melted

FILLING

1 tbsp (8 g) ground cinnamon

¼ cup (50 g) granulated sugar

¼ cup (60 g) light brown sugar

⅓ cup (75 g) vegan butter, at room temperature

Activate the yeast: In a small bowl, add the sugar and yeast to the warm milk and give it a stir. When it doubles in size, 6 to 10 minutes, it is ready.

Meanwhile, in a medium-sized bowl, combine the flour blend, tapioca starch, salt, xanthan gum and baking powder. Blend well and set aside.

In a stand mixer fitted with the paddle attachment, beat the egg whites on medium-high speed for 4 minutes. They should be white and frothy, but not with peaks. Pour the egg whites into a separate small bowl and set aside.

With the stand mixer on the STIR setting, combine 1 of the egg yolks with the melted vegan butter and activated yeast. Allow those to blend, then add the egg whites while still mixing.

Slowly add the flour mixture with the stand mixer on the slowest speed. Blend on low speed until a dough forms, about 30 seconds. Scrape the sides of the bowl with a spatula and blend on low speed for another 30 seconds. Remove the bowl from the mixer, place a clean towel over the bowl and allow it to rest for 5 minutes.

Prepare the filling: In a small bowl, stir together the cinnamon and granulated and brown sugars, then set aside.

Lay plastic wrap on your kitchen counter where you are going to roll out the dough. I give myself a lot of space. Make sure you have enough plastic wrap for the entire piece of dough to be rolled out—it will be 12 x 15 inches (30 x 38 cm).

Place the dough in the middle of the plastic wrap and lay plastic wrap over the top, pressing it down to flatten the dough a little bit. Then, roll the dough out to be ¼ inch (6 mm) thick and to measure 12 x 15 inches (30 x 38 cm). Remove the top layer of the plastic wrap.

(Continued)

PECAN STICKY BUNS (CONTINUED)

¾ cup (170 g) light brown sugar
⅓ cup (80 ml) pure maple syrup
¼ tsp salt
1 cup (110 g) chopped pecans
⅓ cup (75 g) vegan butter, melted

Fill the dough: Gently spread the room-temperature vegan butter over the dough, but leave 1 inch (2.5 cm) around the edges without butter. Sprinkle the cinnamon mixture on top of the butter.

To roll up the dough, take one short end and press about 1 inch (2.5 cm) of it into the filling to secure what will become the center of the cinnamon roll. You will then roll it up all the way by holding the plastic wrap on the same end and lifting up. As you lift, it will roll up on its own, but you will need to press it together occasionally to make sure there isn't too much space between the layers of dough. Do this until it is completely rolled up.

Prepare the topping: In a small bowl, combine the brown sugar, maple syrup, salt and pecans with the melted butter. Pour onto the bottom of a 9 x 13–inch (23 x 33–cm) baking dish.

To cut the rolls, use thread: You will shimmy the thread under the roll and then pull the ends up toward each other; it will slice them perfectly. You want to make the rolls about 1½ inches (4 cm) thick.

Place the cut rolls on top of the topping in the baking dish. Cover with a clean towel and allow them to rise for 30 minutes. Meanwhile, preheat the oven to 350°F (180°C).

After 30 minutes, remove the towel and place the baking dish in the oven. Bake for 30 to 32 minutes, or until the tops are golden and a toothpick inserted into the center of a cinnamon roll comes out clean.

Remove from the oven and allow to cool in the pan for about 15 minutes, then serve warm.

YEAST-RISEN FRIED DONUTS

2¼ tsp (9 g) active dry yeast

¼ cup (50 g) + 1½ tsp (6 g) granulated sugar, divided

½ cup (120 ml) warm water (110°F [43°C])

1 cup (240 ml) warm coconut milk (110°F [43°C])

⅓ cup (75 g) coconut oil, plus 2½ cups (563 g) for frying

⅓ cup (75 g) vegan butter

2 large eggs

Pinch of salt

2 tsp (5 g) xanthan gum

4 cups (640 g) The Best Ever Gluten-Free All-Purpose Flour Blend (page 229)

After going gluten-free, the one thing I craved terribly was a true yeast-risen fried donut. For years, I searched high and low, but was disappointed every time. This was a recipe that I created for myself and others who want a real gluten- and dairy-free donut. I had heard from so many about how none of the recipes they tried turned out well, and I knew I could make one. It actually took many years for me to get these just right. These are the real deal.

Activate the yeast: In a small bowl, add the yeast and 1½ teaspoons (6 g) of granulated sugar to the warm water and give it a stir. Once it doubles in size, 6 to 10 minutes, it is ready.

Meanwhile, in a small saucepan, heat the coconut milk over low heat until warm. Add the coconut oil and vegan butter to the warm milk. Stir to melt. Remove from the heat.

In a stand mixer fitted with the paddle attachment, beat the eggs on medium speed for 4 minutes. Reduce the mixer speed to low and add the activated yeast. Mix for 1 minute.

Add the salt, remaining ¼ cup (50 g) of granulated sugar, xanthan gum and flour blend. Mix for 2 minutes.

Line a baking sheet with parchment paper. Lay some plastic wrap flat on your kitchen counter.

Place ½ cup (120 g) of the dough on the plastic wrap. Add another sheet of plastic wrap over the top of the dough and gently press down to flatten the ball of dough. Repeat this process to use all the dough.

Cut out the donuts with a donut cutter—you should have 10 donuts—and place them 2 inches (5 cm) apart on the prepared baking sheet. Cover the donuts with a clean towel and let them rise for 20 minutes.

(Continued)

YEAST-RISEN FRIED DONUTS (CONTINUED)

MAPLE GLAZE

2 cups (240 g) Grain-Free Powdered Sugar (page 230)

1½ tsp (8 ml) maple extract

1 tsp pure maple syrup

3 tbsp (45 ml) coconut milk

To fry, heat the coconut oil to 275 to 300°F (135 to 150°C) and use a candy thermometer to monitor the temperature. Working in batches, place the donuts in the hot oil and fry for 1 to 1½ minutes per side, just until golden brown. Carefully transfer the cooked donuts to a wire rack and allow them to cool for 20 minutes before frosting.

Prepare the glaze: In a bowl, combine all the glaze ingredients and mix well with a whisk or spoon. Line a wire rack with parchment paper. Working one by one, drop each donut into the glaze mixture and pick it up carefully by placing your index finger into the hole. Lay on the lined rack, glaze side up, and allow the glaze to set for at least 20 minutes before serving. These taste best served the same day.

MY TWO-CENTS

If you do not like coconut, or have an allergy to it, you can use vegetable oil to fry instead.

If your dough turns out sticky and is sticking to the donut cutter, you can dip the donut cutter in water and then cut the dough. Having the cutter wet helps prevent sticking.

If you don't need to be corn-free, you can use corn syrup in place of the maple syrup in the glaze. Corn syrup allows it to stay moist and not dry out as fast.

FROM-SCRATCH BISCUITS AND GRAVY

SERVES 4 OR 5

My mom grew up in the South and biscuits and gravy were something they ate often. This is one recipe my mom has been making for me my entire life. Making gravy wasn't always easy, especially when we were trying to figure out how to make it gluten- and dairy-free. With a few errors, we finally perfected it. My mom helped me get it just right!

BISCUITS

2 cups (320 g) The Best Ever Gluten-Free All-Purpose Flour Blend (page 229)

½ tsp sea salt

Pinch of freshly ground black pepper

1 tsp Paleo Grain-Free Baking Powder (page 231)

½ tsp baking soda

¼ cup (55 g) vegan butter

1 cup (240 ml) coconut milk

1 tbsp (15 ml) cider vinegar

GRAVY

1 (12-oz [340-g]) package bacon

¼ cup (40 g) The Best Ever Gluten-Free All-Purpose Flour Blend (page 229)

2 cups (480 ml) coconut milk

¼ tsp salt

¼ tsp freshly ground black pepper

¼ tsp granulated garlic

Paprika, for garnish

Prepare the biscuits: Preheat the oven to 350°F (180°C). Line a baking sheet with parchment paper.

In a bowl, whisk together the flour blend, salt, pepper, baking powder and baking soda. Add the vegan butter and mash it into the flour mixture with a pastry cutter. Add the coconut milk and cider vinegar and blend with a spoon.

Use an ice-cream scoop to transfer mounds of the dough 2 inches (5 cm) apart on the prepared baking sheet. Bake for about 20 minutes, or until the biscuits are golden brown and a toothpick inserted into the center of a biscuit comes out clean.

While the biscuits bake, prepare the gravy: In a large skillet, fry the bacon over medium heat. Once the bacon is cooked, transfer it to a paper towel–lined plate, but leave all the bacon fat in the pan over medium heat. Add the flour blend to the pan while stirring. Allow the flour to dissolve and then add the coconut milk 1 cup (240 ml) at a time, stirring constantly. As soon as it thickens, 2 to 3 minutes, remove from the heat. Add the salt, pepper and granulated garlic.

Smother the biscuits with the gravy, garnish with paprika and serve with the bacon.

MY TWO-CENTS

You will love these biscuits even without the gravy. They are amazing with butter or jelly.

If you are using regular dairy for this recipe, the measurements are the same. You will want to use whole milk, though.

If your gravy gets thick too fast, lower the heat to low and add a little extra milk.

BREAKFAST ENCHILADA CASSEROLE

SERVES 9

1 (15-oz [425-g]) can black beans, drained and rinsed

1 batch Spanish Cauliflower Rice (page 109)

18 gluten-free tortillas (see page 146 for homemade)

8 large eggs, scrambled

1 lb (455 g) ground sausage

ENCHILADA SAUCE

½ cup plus 2 tbsp (150 ml) avocado oil

⅔ cup (85 g) tapioca starch

⅔ cup (80 g) chili powder

¼ cup (28 g) ground cumin

1 tbsp (9 g) granulated garlic

½ tsp sea salt

¼ tsp freshly ground black pepper

2 cups (475 ml) tomato sauce

6 cups (1.4 L) chicken or vegetable broth

2 tbsp (4 g) dried oregano

I love Mexican food for breakfast. As a teenager and young adult, I used to frequent a local Mexican restaurant that served brunch. It was absolutely amazing. Nothing beats eggs, meat, tortillas, rice and beans for breakfast. I dreamed up this recipe one night when I was lying in bed trying to fall asleep; I actually do that a lot. I was so excited to make this, and it is delicious!

Have the beans, cauliflower rice, tortillas and scrambled eggs ready to go. In a skillet, brown the ground sausage, 5 to 8 minutes, and set aside.

Prepare the sauce: In a large, deep skillet, heat the avocado oil over medium heat. Add the tapioca starch, chili powder, cumin, granulated garlic, salt and black pepper. Stir to form a paste. Add the tomato sauce and broth, 1 cup (240 ml) at a time, stirring vigorously. Continue to stir and the sauce will start to thicken. Once it thickens, lower the heat to a simmer and cook for 5 more minutes. Sprinkle the oregano onto the sauce and stir.

Preheat the oven to 400°F (200°C).

Pour enough sauce onto the bottom of a 9 x 13–inch (23 x 33–cm) baking dish to cover it generously, then layer in 6 tortillas, one-half each of the cauliflower rice, beans, eggs and sausage, then 6 more tortillas, half of the remaining sauce, the remainder of the cauliflower rice, beans, eggs and sausage, finally 6 tortillas and then the remainder of the sauce. Bake, uncovered, for 25 to 30 minutes; the sauce should be bubbling.

MY TWO-CENTS

You can switch things in this recipe to make it yours. Any bean will work and you can use a different meat in place of the ground sausage.

I encourage you to save this sauce recipe and use it to make dinner enchiladas, or to pour onto burritos. It is truly delicious!

CHOCOLATE WAFFLES

MAKES 7 WAFFLES

These chocolate waffles are one of my kids' favorite breakfasts. What is better than decadent chocolate for breakfast? I am such a sucker for a good waffle, and these are the ones I cannot resist. I love sliced strawberries, or any seasonal fruit, on top. They are also the perfect base for making a delicious ice-cream sundae.

2 cups (320 g) The Best Ever Gluten-Free All-Purpose Flour Blend (page 229)

¼ cup (60 g) light brown sugar

¼ cup (28 g) unsweetened cocoa powder

1 tbsp (12 g) Paleo Grain-Free Baking Powder (page 231)

2 tbsp (14 g) flaxseed meal

3 large eggs

1 tsp vanilla extract

1½ cups (355 ml) coconut milk

¼ cup (55 g) coconut oil, melted

1 cup (175 g) vegan chocolate chips

Maple syrup or honey, for drizzling

You can make the batter with a hand mixer or even a stand mixer, but I use a wooden spoon. In a medium-sized bowl, combine the flour blend, brown sugar, cocoa powder, baking powder and flaxseed meal and mix until blended together. Add the eggs, vanilla and coconut milk. Stir until a batter has formed and all the lumps are gone. Pour in the melted coconut oil while stirring it into the batter; blend well. Fold in the chocolate chips.

Heat a waffle maker and add ½ cup (120 ml) of batter per waffle. Cook according to the manufacturer's instructions; mine took about 4 minutes to cook.

Serve with maple syrup or honey.

LEMON-BLUEBERRY PANCAKES

MAKES 15 PANCAKES

2 cups (320 g) The Best Ever Gluten-Free All-Purpose Flour Blend (page 229)

¼ cup (56 g) coconut sugar

1 tbsp (12 g) Paleo Grain-Free Baking Powder (page 231)

Pinch of salt

2 tbsp (14 g) flaxseed meal

2 large eggs

1 tsp vanilla extract

2 tbsp (12 g) fresh lemon zest

2 tbsp (30 ml) fresh lemon juice

1 cup (240 ml) coconut milk

¼ cup (60 ml) melted coconut oil

1½ cups (218 g) blueberries

Honey or pure maple syrup, for serving

Pancakes are a family staple of ours, but regular pancakes can get boring. I decided to try lemon with blueberry for a fun burst of flavor. Not only do these gluten- and dairy-free pancakes taste amazing, but they are easy to make and beautiful to look at. I love serving these at brunch with Champagne.

In a large bowl, combine the flour blend, coconut sugar, baking powder, salt and flaxseed meal, then mix together until blended. Add the eggs, vanilla, lemon zest and juice and coconut milk and mix well. Blend in the melted coconut oil. Fold in the blueberries last.

Heat a nonstick skillet over medium heat and pour in ¼ cup (60 ml) of batter per pancake. Cook for 2 minutes on the first side and for 1 to 2 minutes on the second side.

Enjoy with honey or maple syrup drizzled over the top.

MY TWO-CENTS

You can use regular sugar in place of the coconut sugar, if needed.

These store in the fridge for about 3 days, so they are perfect to make on the weekend and to enjoy during the week.

I had a friend make this with a store-bought 1:1 flour and they turned out incredibly thick. The flavor was still great, but a thicker texture. Please remember that your choice of gluten-free all-purpose flour makes a huge difference. I recommend using my blend in this book.

FRENCH TOAST CASSEROLE

SERVES 6

Nonstick spray
6 large eggs
2 cups (475 ml) coconut milk
1 tsp ground cinnamon
¼ tsp ground nutmeg
1 loaf Sliceable Sandwich Bread
(page 130), cut into 1-inch
(2.5-cm) cubes

CRUMB TOPPING

¼ cup (40 g) The Best Ever
Gluten-Free All-Purpose Flour
Blend (page 229)
¼ cup (60 g) light brown sugar
¼ tsp ground nutmeg
1 tsp ground cinnamon
¼ cup (55 g) vegan butter

Fresh berries, for serving
Pure maple syrup, for serving

Nothing beats a beautiful and elegant French toast casserole for a fun brunch or Sunday breakfast. The crumb topping brings an extra element to this flavorful casserole. I love topping this with fresh fruit and serving with eggs and bacon for a complete brunch or breakfast.

Preheat the oven to 350°F (180°C). Spray a 9 x 13–inch (23 x 33–cm) baking dish with nonstick spray.

In a large bowl, whisk together the eggs and coconut milk. Stir in the cinnamon and nutmeg. Add the cubed bread and let it soak up the mixture for 10 to 15 minutes.

Pour the bread into the prepared baking dish.

Prepare the crumb topping: In a bowl, combine all the topping ingredients and blend with a pastry blender, then sprinkle on top of the bread. Bake for 55 minutes, or until the top is golden brown and a butter knife inserted into the center comes out clean.

Serve with fresh berries and maple syrup.

MY TWO-CENTS
In a pinch, you can use a store-bought loaf of gluten-free bread, but this homemade bread truly makes it a special treat.

INCREDIBLE EGGS BENEDICT

I am madly in love with a good eggs Benedict. It has always been one of my favorites, and I have only found one place that makes this gluten- and dairy-free. I was honestly intimidated about making this for many years, but it was actually not as hard as I expected it to be. It's a true treat, and this is something I make for myself when I need a little extra love.

HOLLANDAISE SAUCE
3 large egg yolks
1½ tbsp (23 ml) water
1½ tbsp (23 ml) fresh lemon juice
¾ cup (167 g) vegan butter
½ tsp salt
½ tsp ground white pepper
Pinch of cayenne pepper

2 tbsp (30 ml) white vinegar, for boiling water
4 large eggs
4 slices Sliceable Sandwich Bread (page 130)
4 slices ham or Canadian bacon

Prepare the sauce: In a saucepan, whisk together the egg yolks, water and lemon juice. Heat over low heat, whisking constantly. Add the vegan butter, 1 tablespoon (14 g) at a time, whisking constantly, until all of it has melted and blended in nicely. Remove from the heat and season with the salt, white pepper and cayenne. Set aside.

Poach the eggs: Poaching eggs can take a little practice. In a large saucepan, bring 2 quarts (1.9 L) of water plus the white vinegar to a boil. Once you have a nice roaring boil, crack 1 egg into a ladle, stir the water with a wooden spoon and then dunk the egg-filled ladle into the middle of the funnel the spoon created. Tip the egg out and let it cook for 4 to 6 minutes. Use the ladle to remove the cooked egg. Repeat with the remaining eggs, poaching them one at a time.

Build your eggs Benedict: You can use a cookie cutter to make the bread slices look pretty. Take a slice of bread and place a slice of ham on top. Place the poached egg on top of the ham and then pour the delicious sauce over the poached egg. Repeat until you have 4 eggs Benedict. Serve warm.

MY TWO-CENTS
You can always use regular butter if this doesn't need to be dairy-free.

Feel free to sprinkle a little ground paprika on top of the eggs Benedict, if you would like.

FRIED APPLE FRITTERS

MAKES ABOUT 2
DOZEN FRITTERS

2¼ tsp (9 g) active dry yeast

¼ cup (50 g) + 1½ tsp (6 g) granulated sugar, divided

½ cup (120 ml) warm water (110°F [43°C])

1 cup (240 ml) warm coconut milk (110°F [43°C])

⅓ cup (75 g) vegan butter

2⅔ cups (600 g) coconut oil, divided

2 large eggs

½ cup (115 g) light brown sugar

1 tsp ground cinnamon

1 tsp vanilla extract

Pinch of salt

2 tsp (5 g) xanthan gum

4 cups (640 g) The Best Ever Gluten-Free All-Purpose Flour Blend (page 229)

4 cups (600 g) peeled, cored and small-diced apples

CINNAMON GLAZE

½ cup (60 g) Grain-Free Powdered Sugar (page 230)

1 tsp vanilla extract

½ tsp ground cinnamon

1 tbsp (15 ml) coconut milk

Nothing beats a freshly fried apple fritter. Once I perfected the Yeast-Risen Fried Donuts recipe (page 167), I knew I could do apple fritters. The best part is they are even easier than the donuts. The lightly crisp outside with a soft and fluffy center is like deep-fried heaven. The cinnamon glaze makes this a true treat.

Activate the yeast: In a small bowl, add the yeast and 1½ teaspoons (6 g) of granulated sugar to the warm water and give it a stir. Once it doubles in size, 5 to 10 minutes, it is ready.

In a saucepan, warm the milk over low heat and add the vegan butter and ⅓ cup (75 g) coconut oil to the warm milk. Allow the butter and oil to melt into the warm milk and then stir to combine. Remove it from the stove and set aside.

In a stand mixer fitted with the paddle attachment, beat the eggs on medium speed for 4 minutes. With the mixer off, add the activated yeast and warm milk mixture and blend on low speed for 1 minute. Add the remaining ¼ cup (50 g) of granulated sugar, brown sugar, cinnamon and vanilla. Blend for 30 seconds. Reduce the mixer speed to low and add the salt, xanthan gum, flour blend and apples. Mix well on low speed for a few minutes, turn off the mixer and scrape down the sides, then mix again on low speed for 30 seconds. Remove the bowl from the mixer and cover with a clean towel. Place in a warm place and allow the dough to rise for 30 minutes.

Fry the fritters: In a large skillet or Dutch oven (I prefer a Dutch oven), heat the remaining coconut oil; the sweet spot is 275 to 300°F (135 to 150°C). Use a candy thermometer to monitor this. Have ready a wire rack or a baking sheet lined with paper towels.

Scoop some dough out of the bowl (I used a ¼-cup [60-ml] measuring cup for this) and gently drop it into the hot oil. These do not need to look perfect, so don't worry about that. Working in batches, fry them for 1½ to 2 minutes per side, maybe a little more depending on the size. You want a nice golden brown fritter. Remove the fritters from the hot oil when they are done and allow the oil to drain either on the rack or on the prepared baking sheet.

Allow the fritters to cool for about 15 minutes.

Prepare the glaze: In a small bowl, combine all the glaze ingredients and stir well. Drizzle the glaze on top of the cooled fritters and serve!

GRAIN-FREE GRANOLA

I love making our own granola because nothing beats the flavor. You can personalize this however you would like by swapping out the nuts and dried fruits for your own favorites. You can even add your favorite chocolate chips if you want. This is excellent with yogurt, on top of ice cream or eaten by the handful.

MAKES ABOUT 7 CUPS (1.1 KG)

1 cup (110 g) slivered almonds
1 cup (100 g) walnuts
1 cup (140 g) cashew pieces
1½ cups (128 g) shredded coconut
1 cup (120 g) dried cranberries
1 cup (120 g) dried cherries
1 cup (100 g) almond flour
¼ cup (28 g) flaxseed meal
½ tsp ground cinnamon
¼ tsp ground nutmeg
½ cup (170 g) honey
½ cup (120 ml) melted coconut oil

Preheat the oven to 350°F (180°C). Line a baking sheet with parchment paper.

In a large bowl, combine the almonds, walnuts, cashews, coconut, cranberries, cherries, almond flour, flaxseed meal, cinnamon and nutmeg and mix well. Drizzle the honey and coconut oil all over the top and then mix again to coat all the nuts and fruit.

Pour the mixture evenly onto the prepared baking sheet, making it as flat as possible. Bake for 24 minutes, or until golden.

Remove from the oven, allow to cool completely, then break into pieces. Store in an airtight container for up to a week.

CLASSIC ZUCCHINI BREAD

MAKES 1 LOAF

½ tsp coconut oil, for pan
2 large eggs
¼ cup (50 g) granulated sugar
¼ cup (60 g) light brown sugar
½ cup (125 g) applesauce
1 tsp vanilla extract
1½ cups (180 g) grated zucchini
⅓ cup (80 ml) melted coconut oil
1½ tsp (3 g) ground cinnamon
1 tsp xanthan gum
½ tsp baking soda
½ tsp Paleo Grain-Free Baking Powder (page 231)
Pinch of salt
1½ cups (240 g) The Best Ever Gluten-Free All-Purpose Flour Blend (page 229)

My grandma would make zucchini bread a few times a year. I remember loving the smell while it baked and also when it was fresh out of the oven. It was always so moist and full of perfect flavor. When I re-created this recipe, I wanted to feel that childhood joy again and share it with my family. The loaf does exactly that. I also love sneaking in vegetables whenever I can, without telling the kids.

Preheat the oven to 325°F (165°C). Oil a 5 x 9–inch (12 x 23–cm) loaf pan with the coconut oil.

In a stand mixer fitted with the paddle attachment, combine the eggs, granulated and brown sugars, applesauce and vanilla and mix for 30 seconds on medium-low speed. With the mixer still on, add the zucchini, melted coconut oil and cinnamon, then mix for 30 seconds. Reduce the mixer speed to low and add the xanthan gum, baking soda, baking powder, salt and flour blend. Mix on medium speed for 1 minute, scraping the sides of the bowl halfway through.

Pour the batter into the prepared loaf pan. Bake for 55 to 60 minutes, or until a butter knife inserted into the center comes out clean.

Allow to cool in the pan for about 25 minutes before removing.

MY TWO-CENTS

My grandma would insist this recipe have walnuts in it, but my kids insist that it does not. Feel free to stir in 1 cup (100 g) of walnuts before pouring into the loaf pan, if you like.

THE BEST BANANA BREAD

MAKES 1 LOAF

½ tsp coconut oil, for pan
1 large egg
½ cup (100 g) sugar
1 tsp vanilla extract
⅓ cup (82 g) applesauce
2 ripe bananas
⅓ cup (80 ml) melted coconut oil
½ tsp ground cinnamon
Pinch of ground nutmeg
Pinch of salt
1 tsp xanthan gum
1 tsp baking soda
½ tsp Paleo Grain-Free Baking Powder (page 231)
1½ cups (240 g) The Best Ever Gluten-Free All-Purpose Flour Blend (page 229)

While growing up and even as an adult, I enjoyed my grandma's banana bread. After going gluten-free, I knew I would have to re-create her banana bread and this one is spot on! This moist, flavorful loaf tastes just like the one your grandma made while you were growing up—minus the gluten and dairy. My kids go crazy for it whenever I make it, and sometimes I like to add chocolate chips, walnuts or pecans to the batter.

Preheat the oven to 350°F (180°C). Oil a 5 x 9–inch (12 x 23–cm) loaf pan with the coconut oil.

In a stand mixer fitted with the paddle attachment, combine the egg, sugar, vanilla, applesauce and bananas on medium-low speed. Increase the speed to medium and mix for 2 minutes. Add the melted coconut oil and mix to blend it into the batter.

Reduce the speed to low and add the cinnamon, nutmeg, salt, xanthan gum, baking soda and baking powder, incorporating them into the mixture.

Add the flour blend, increase the speed to medium and mix for 2 to 3 more minutes, scraping the sides of the bowl with a spatula halfway through.

Pour the batter into the prepared loaf pan. Bake for 50 minutes, or until a butter knife inserted into the center comes out clean.

Remove from the oven and allow to cool for 20 minutes, then pop the loaf out of the pan. You can use a butter knife to separate the loaf from the sides of the pan, if it needs a little help. Allow the loaf to cool for an additional 20 to 30 minutes before slicing open.

MY TWO-CENTS
Feel free to mix in up to 1 cup (100 g) of nuts or (175 g) vegan chocolate chips to the batter before pouring into the loaf pan.

Sweet Treats

One of the biggest hurdles when going gluten-free is learning how to bake. Gluten-free baked goods often turn out dense and grainy. I was tired of not enjoying my favorite desserts and treats, so I set out to learn how to make gluten-free baked goods fluffy, moist and delicious. All of these dessert recipes are going to turn into family favorites. I serve them to all my friends and family for every gathering and special occasion. I remember one year, for my son's birthday, I served a store-bought gluten-containing cake to the guests and made gluten-free cupcakes for us—my family was so disappointed that I didn't make a homemade cake for everyone. In fact, my family fought over who got to take the leftover cupcakes home after the party. Know that all of these treats will taste exactly like you expect them to. You will be able to share them all with confidence! In this chapter, you will find fabulous cakes, including Perfect Carrot Cake (page 217), German Chocolate Cake (page 208) and traditional yellow cake (page 207). There are pies, including Chocolate-Coconut Cream Pie (page 222) and Cherry Pie Tartlets (page 218). As for cookies, there are Cinnamon-Raisin Oatmeal and Double Chocolate Chip (pages 203 and 200) and Fudgy Pecan Brownies (page 195). The Southern-Style Peach Cobbler (page 192) is one of my favorite desserts.

SOUTHERN-STYLE PEACH COBBLER

SERVES 8

VEGAN

PEACH FILLING

6 cups (1 kg) peeled, pitted and thinly sliced yellow peaches

2 tsp (10 ml) fresh lemon juice

¼ cup (60 g) light brown sugar

¼ cup (50 g) granulated sugar

¼ tsp ground cinnamon

¼ tsp ground nutmeg

1 tbsp (8 g) tapioca starch

TOPPING

1¾ cups (280 g) The Best Ever Gluten-Free All-Purpose Flour Blend (page 229)

¼ cup (60 g) light brown sugar

½ cup (100 g) granulated sugar, divided

2 tsp (8 g) Paleo Grain-Free Baking Powder (page 231)

¼ tsp sea salt

1 tsp xanthan gum

½ cup (112 g) vegan butter, chilled

½ cup (120 ml) boiling water

2 tsp (5 g) ground cinnamon

After we bought our first home, my best friend moved down the street. She was blessed with a peach tree and supplied me with endless peaches. We have both moved since, but I miss her peach tree. I'll never forget how one of the first recipes I created gluten- and dairy-free was peach cobbler. This cobbler is absolutely delicious and one of my favorite summer desserts.

Preheat the oven to 350°F (180°C).

Prepare the filling: In a large bowl, toss the peaches with the lemon juice, brown and granulated sugars, cinnamon, nutmeg and tapioca starch. Pour into a 9 x 13–inch (23 x 33–cm) baking dish and bake for 15 minutes.

Meanwhile, prepare the topping: In a medium-sized bowl, combine the flour blend, brown sugar, ¼ cup (50 g) granulated sugar, baking powder, salt and xanthan gum. Whisk well. With a cheese grater, grate the vegan butter on top and toss it around into the dry mixture. Pour in the boiling water and stir to blend.

Prepare the cinnamon sugar sprinkle: In a small bowl, stir together the remaining granulated sugar and cinnamon.

Remove the peach filling from the oven. Use an ice-cream scoop to scoop the topping evenly over the top, then sprinkle the cinnamon-sugar all over the top. Place back in the oven and bake for another 25 to 30 minutes, or until the top has a beautiful golden brown crust.

FUDGY PECAN BROWNIES

MAKES 9 TO 12 BROWNIES

Coconut oil, for pan
1½ cups (240 g) The Best Ever Gluten-Free All-Purpose Flour Blend (page 229)
1 cup (86 g) unsweetened cocoa powder
1 tsp salt
1 tsp Paleo Grain-Free Baking Powder (page 231)
¾ tsp xanthan gum
1½ cups (300 g) granulated sugar
¾ cup (170 g) light brown sugar
1 tbsp (15 ml) vanilla extract
4 large eggs
1 cup (240 ml) melted coconut oil
1 cup (175 g) vegan chocolate chips
1 cup (100 g) pecans, divided

Brownies were a recipe that was hard to perfect while being gluten- and dairy-free. I tried for a while and then gave up. I am glad I went back to work, though, because these are so delicious! These have the perfect crunch around the edges with a delicious soft center. One of our favorite ways to enjoy these is with a big scoop of ice cream on top.

Preheat the oven to 350°F (180°C). Oil a 9-inch (23-cm) square baking pan with coconut oil.

In a large bowl, combine the flour blend, cocoa powder, salt, baking powder and xanthan gum. Stir until well combined. In your stand mixer fitted with the paddle attachment, combine the granulated and brown sugar, vanilla and eggs, then mix on medium-low speed for 1 minute. Add the melted coconut oil while the mixer is going and allow it to blend through. Slowly add the flour mixture, 1 cup (160 g) at a time, and mix on medium speed for 2 minutes, scraping the sides of the bowl halfway through. Fold in the chocolate chips and ¾ cup (75 g) of the pecans and mix on low speed for about 30 seconds.

Pour into the prepared baking pan. Scatter the remaining ¼ cup (25 g) of pecans on top for aesthetics, if desired. Bake for 55 to 60 minutes, or until a butter knife inserted into the center comes out clean.

Remove from the oven and allow the brownies to cool in the pan for at least 20 minutes before cutting.

MY TWO-CENTS
You can use walnuts instead of pecans, if you like, or omit the nuts altogether if you have a nut allergy.

MAGIC COOKIE BARS

MAKES 6 TO 9 BARS

VEGAN

Coconut oil, for pan
1½ cups (135 g) gluten-free graham cracker crumbs
3 tbsp (45 ml) melted coconut oil
1½ cups (263 g) vegan chocolate chips
½ cup (50 g) walnuts
2 cups (186 g) shredded coconut
1 (11.25-oz [320-g]) can sweetened condensed coconut milk

These squares of amazingness are absolutely magic even while being gluten- and dairy-free. These are a childhood favorite of mine and remind me of being a child in my grandma Olga's kitchen. After going dairy-free, I thought these were a part of my past, but when I found condensed coconut milk at the store, I knew I could finally create this recipe again! I love this recipe because these bars are really easy and quick to make, but look and taste like they took hours.

Preheat the oven to 350°F (180°C). Oil a 9-inch (23-cm) square baking dish with coconut oil.

In a medium-sized bowl, combine the graham cracker crumbs and melted coconut oil, then pour the mixture onto the bottom of the baking dish. Press the crumbs into the dish firmly. Sprinkle the chocolate chips evenly over the crumb mixture, then the walnuts and coconut. If the condensed coconut milk is very thick, place the can in a bowl of hot water for 5 to 10 minutes to help melt it a bit. Pour the condensed coconut milk evenly over the top of the mixture in the baking dish. Bake for 25 minutes, or until the top is golden brown.

Remove from the oven and allow to cool for about 30 minutes, then cut into squares and serve.

MY TWO-CENTS

You can use regular sweetened condensed milk if this does not need to be dairy-free. You can also leave out the walnuts, if desired, or use pecans instead.

RASPBERRY FRUIT BARS

MAKES 15 BARS

Coconut oil, for pan

1½ cups (240 g) The Best Ever Gluten-Free All-Purpose Flour Blend (page 229)

½ cup (100 g) sugar

Pinch of salt

1 tsp vanilla extract

¼ tsp almond extract

¼ cup (55 g) firm coconut oil

1 tbsp (15 ml) avocado oil

1 large egg

2 (17-oz [482-g]) jars raspberry preserves

1 cup (120 g) chopped walnuts

On a night out with my best friend, we stopped at a gluten-free bakery and she ordered a raspberry bar. She kept talking about it for days after that, so I decided to create a fruit bar recipe. The preserves make this easy to put together and the crumb topping makes it a comforting yet simple treat.

Preheat the oven to 350°F (180°C). Oil a 9 x 13–inch (23 x 33–cm) baking dish with coconut oil.

Prepare the crust: In a medium-sized bowl, combine the flour blend, sugar, salt, vanilla and almond extract. Add the coconut oil, avocado oil and egg, then cut it into the mixture with a pastry blender, kneading with your hands if necessary. Remove ½ cup (80 g) of the crust mixture and set aside to use for the topping.

Press the crust mixture into the prepared baking dish. You want the crust to be nice and firm on the bottom. Spoon the preserves over the crust and then spread it evenly (I use a butter knife to do this). Add the chopped walnuts to the reserved crust mixture, then sprinkle evenly over the preserves.

Bake on the middle rack for 30 minutes. The crust should be golden brown.

Remove from the oven and allow it to cool to room temperature, then refrigerate at least 4 hours or overnight before serving.

Store in the refrigerator as the bars will soften if left out. These taste best when eaten in the first 2 days.

MY TWO-CENTS
You can use any flavor preserves in place of raspberry.

DOUBLE CHOCOLATE CHIP COOKIES

MAKES 3 DOZEN COOKIES

1½ cups (337 g) vegan butter
¼ cup (60 g) light brown sugar
1½ cups (300 g) granulated sugar
1 tsp vanilla extract
3 large eggs
¾ cup (65 g) unsweetened cocoa powder
1½ tsp (7 g) baking soda
1 tsp Paleo Grain-Free Baking Powder (page 231)
2 tsp (5 g) xanthan gum
¼ tsp salt
2½ cups (400 g) The Best Ever Gluten-Free All-Purpose Flour Blend (page 229)
1½ cups (263 g) vegan chocolate chips

These fluffy cookies have a light crunch on the outside, but inside they are soft and chewy. They are truly the perfect chocolate chip cookie to enjoy anytime. These are one of my family's favorite cookies, even for members who are not gluten-free. When I make them, I bake a dozen and then freeze the rest of the dough for freshly baked cookies in a pinch. I love having the dough on hand for unexpected guests.

Preheat the oven to 350°F (180°C). Line a baking sheet with parchment paper.

In a stand mixer fitted with the paddle attachment, cream together the vegan butter and brown and granulated sugars on medium-low speed. Add the vanilla and eggs and mix on medium-high speed until the mixture fluffs up nicely, 2 to 3 minutes. Add the cocoa powder and mix for 1 minute. Add the baking soda, baking powder, xanthan gum, salt and flour blend. Mix for 3 minutes on medium speed, scraping the sides of the bowl halfway through. Add the chocolate chips and mix for 15 to 20 seconds, just until the chocolate chips are blended through the mixture.

Use a 1½-tablespoon (22-ml) cookie scoop to drop the dough about 2 inches (5 cm) apart onto the parchment paper. For a fluffier cookie, refrigerate the dough for 20 to 30 minutes prior to scooping onto the baking sheet. Bake for 14 minutes, or until the center is cooked through.

Remove from the oven and allow to cool on a wire rack for 20 minutes before serving.

MY TWO-CENTS
This dough freezes perfectly. Simply place the balls of cookie dough on parchment paper and store in a freezer bag. When ready to eat, remove from the freezer and bake, without thawing, at 350°F (180°C) for 17 minutes. They come out perfect!

CINNAMON-RAISIN OATMEAL COOKIES

MAKES 3 DOZEN COOKIES

Oatmeal cookies are a staple recipe that everyone grew up eating. I loved my grandma's recipe, and it was always a treat when she made oatmeal cookies, so adding these to the book was very important to me. They taste just like hers. You will love how soft and chewy they are.

2 large eggs
1 cup (225 g) vegan butter
1 cup (225 g) light brown sugar
½ cup (100 g) granulated sugar
1 tbsp (15 ml) vanilla extract
¼ tsp salt
1 tsp baking soda
1½ tsp (4 g) xanthan gum
¼ tsp ground nutmeg
1¼ tsp (3 g) ground cinnamon
1 cup (100 g) certified gluten-free oat flour
1 cup (160 g) The Best Ever Gluten-Free All-Purpose Flour Blend (page 229)
2 cups (160 g) certified gluten-free rolled oats
1 cup (145 g) raisins

Preheat the oven to 350°F (180°C). Line a baking sheet with parchment paper.

In a stand mixer fitted with the paddle attachment, cream the eggs and vegan butter on medium-low speed for 1 minute. Add the brown and granulated sugars and vanilla, then mix well. Add the salt, baking soda, xanthan gum, nutmeg, cinnamon and oat flour. Blend for about 30 seconds and then add the flour blend. Mix for 1 minute. Add the oats and blend on medium speed for 3 minutes, scraping the sides of the bowl halfway through. Once it is done mixing, fold in the raisins.

Spoon the dough 2 inches (5 cm) apart onto the prepared baking pan. I love using a cookie scoop for this, but if you don't have one, use about 1 tablespoon (15 g) of cookie dough per cookie. Bake for 17 minutes, or until the outside is golden and the center is cooked through.

Remove from the oven, transfer the cookies to a wire rack and allow to cool for about 20 minutes before serving.

MY TWO-CENTS

If you don't like raisins, chocolate chips are amazing in this recipe.

You can always use regular butter in place of the vegan butter, if you don't need it to be dairy-free.

You can make your own oat flour by simply placing oats in a high-speed blender or food processor and blending until they turn into a flour. This usually takes 2 to 3 minutes.

LEMON CAKE
WITH LEMON BUTTERCREAM

MAKES ONE
8" (20-CM)
2-LAYER CAKE

Coconut oil, for pans
½ cup (112 g) vegan butter
1½ cups (300 g) granulated sugar
4 large egg whites
3 tbsp (18 g) fresh lemon zest
3 tbsp (45 ml) fresh lemon juice
2 tsp (10 ml) lemon extract
1¼ cups (355 ml) coconut milk
2 tbsp (30 ml) melted coconut oil
Pinch of salt
1 tsp xanthan gum
2 tsp (8 g) Paleo Grain-Free Baking Powder (page 231)
2 tsp (9 g) baking soda
2½ cups (400 g) The Best Ever Gluten-Free All-Purpose Flour Blend (page 229)

LEMON BUTTERCREAM

½ cup (112 g) vegan butter
½ cup (112 g) vegetable shortening
2½ cups (300 g) Grain-Free Powdered Sugar (page 230)
2 tbsp (12 g) fresh lemon zest
2½ tbsp (22 ml) fresh lemon juice

Lemon is a delicate flavor that is so enjoyable. This light cake has the perfect balance of citrus and sweetness.

Preheat the oven to 350°F (180°C). Oil two 8-inch (20-cm) round cake pans with coconut oil.

In a stand mixer fitted with the paddle attachment, cream together the vegan butter, granulated sugar and egg whites on medium speed until well blended. With the mixer on, add the lemon zest and juice and lemon extract. Once blended in, add the coconut milk and melted coconut oil and blend for 1 minute. Add the salt, xanthan gum, baking powder, baking soda and flour blend. Mix on medium-high speed for 4 minutes, scraping the sides of the bowl halfway through. The batter should have a nice pudding-like consistency.

Divide the batter evenly between the prepared cake pans. Bake for 25 to 30 minutes, or until a butter knife inserted into the center comes out clean.

Remove the cakes from the oven and let them cool in the pans for 20 minutes. Then remove the cakes from the pans, transfer to a wire rack and let cool for at least 1 to 2 hours before frosting. You can refrigerate the layers and frost them the next day, or up to 2 days later.

Prepare the buttercream: In the stand mixer, fitted with the paddle attachment, combine the vegan butter, shortening and powdered sugar. Mix on medium speed for 1 minute. Add the lemon zest and juice. Increase the speed to medium-high and beat until fluffy, about 3 minutes, scraping the sides of the bowl halfway through to thoroughly incorporate the sugar.

Place one-third of the frosting on top of one cake layer and spread evenly. Place the second layer on top, add one-third of the frosting to that and spread evenly. Use the remaining frosting to cover the sides of the cake.

You can make and ice the cake and then serve the next day, but store in the refrigerator.

MY TWO-CENTS
If you are planning to not only frost but also to decorate and pipe the entire cake, you might need to double the lemon buttercream recipe.

YELLOW CELEBRATION CAKE
WITH FUDGE FROSTING

MAKES ONE
8" (20-CM)
3-LAYER CAKE

Coconut oil, for pans
1 cup (225 g) vegan butter
1¾ cups (350 g) granulated sugar
1 tbsp (15 ml) vanilla extract
2 large eggs
2 large egg yolks
1 cup (240 ml) coconut milk
¼ cup (61 g) vegan vanilla yogurt
1 tsp xanthan gum
2 tsp (8 g) Paleo Grain-Free Baking Powder (page 231)
2 tsp (9 g) baking soda
Pinch of salt
2½ cups (400 g) The Best Ever Gluten-Free All-Purpose Flour Blend (page 229)

FUDGE FROSTING

1 cup (225 g) vegan butter
1 cup (86 g) unsweetened cocoa powder
2 tsp (10 ml) vanilla extract
⅔ cup (160 ml) boiling water
8 cups (960 g) Grain-Free Powdered Sugar (page 230)

This cake is delicious and has a tasty and decadent fudge frosting smothered all over it. This moist cake will be perfect for all your celebrations.

Preheat the oven to 350°F (180°C). Oil three 8-inch (20-cm) round cake pans with coconut oil.

In a stand mixer fitted with the paddle attachment, combine the butter, granulated sugar, vanilla, eggs and egg yolks and mix on medium-low speed for 1 minute to blend, scraping the sides with a spatula halfway through. Add the coconut milk and yogurt and blend on medium speed for 1 minute. Reduce the speed to low and add the xanthan gum, baking powder, baking soda, salt and flour blend. Increase the speed to medium-high and mix for 6 to 8 minutes, scraping the sides of the bowl halfway through. The batter should have a pudding-like consistency. Divide the batter evenly among the prepared pans. Bake for 22 to 25 minutes, or until a butter knife inserted into the center comes out clean.

Remove the cakes from the oven and let them cool in the pans for 20 minutes. Remove from the pans, transfer to a wire rack and let cool for at least 1 to 2 hours before frosting. You can refrigerate the layers and frost them the next day or up to 2 days later.

Prepare the frosting: In the stand mixer fitted with the paddle attachment, mix the vegan butter and cocoa powder on low speed until well blended. Add the vanilla and boiling water. Once the butter is melted, turn off the mixer and scrape the sides of the bowl. Then, with the mixer on medium speed, add the powdered sugar 1 cup (120 g) at a time and mix for 2 to 4 minutes on medium-high speed, scraping the sides of the bowl halfway through.

Ensure the cakes are completely cool before frosting. Place one-third of the frosting on one cake layer and spread evenly. Place a second layer on top and spread evenly with one-third of the frosting. Place the last layer on top and evenly spread the remaining frosting on top. I don't typically frost the sides of this, but if you would like to, you can use one-quarter of the frosting to top each layer and the remaining frosting for the sides.

MY TWO-CENTS
You can always use regular dairy in place of vegan options, if this does not need to be dairy-free.

GERMAN CHOCOLATE CAKE

WITH COCONUT-PECAN FROSTING

MAKES ONE
8" (20-CM)
3-LAYER CAKE

Coconut oil, for pans
1 cup (240 ml) water
1½ cups (300 g) sugar, divided
4 large eggs, separated
1 tbsp (15 ml) melted coconut oil
½ cup (112 g) vegan butter
1 tbsp (15 ml) vanilla extract
1 cup (240 ml) coconut milk
Pinch of salt
2 tsp (8 g) Paleo Grain-Free Baking Powder (page 231)
2 tsp (9 g) baking soda
1 tsp xanthan gum
1 cup (86 g) unsweetened cocoa powder
2½ cups (400 g) The Best Ever Gluten-Free All-Purpose Flour Blend (page 229)

German chocolate cake with coconut pecan frosting has always been one of my absolute favorite cake flavors. I remember eating it often while growing up, but the cake was always from a box mix with the premade frosting from a can. Can you believe I never made this frosting from scratch until I went gluten- and dairy-free? It is so easy and delicious, and my family loves it so much that they all have been requesting it for their birthday cakes.

Preheat the oven to 350°F (180°C). Oil three 8-inch (20-cm) round baking pans well with coconut oil.

In a saucepan, combine the water with ½ cup (100 g) of the sugar and bring to a low boil, heat for 2 to 3 minutes, just until the sugar is dissolved, then remove from the heat and allow the mixture to return to room temperature.

In a stand mixer fitted with the whisk attachment, beat the egg whites on high speed for 3 minutes. Remove the egg whites from the bowl and set aside in a separate small bowl. In the mixer bowl, combine the remaining 1 cup (200 g) of sugar, cooled water mixture, melted coconut oil, vegan butter, vanilla, coconut milk and egg yolks. Blend on low speed for 1 minute. While that mixture is blending, in a separate bowl, whisk together the salt, baking powder, baking soda, xanthan gum, cocoa powder and flour blend. With the mixer still on low speed, add the dry mixture to the wet mixture slowly so you don't make a mess. Allow to blend together, then gently fold in the beaten egg whites. Blend for another minute.

Divide the batter evenly among the prepared baking pans and bake for 20 minutes, or until a butter knife inserted into the center comes out clean.

Remove the cakes from the oven and let them cool in the pans for 20 minutes. Remove from the pans, transfer to a wire rack and let cool for at least 1 to 2 hours before frosting. You can refrigerate the cakes and frost them the next day or up to 2 days later.

(Continued)

GERMAN CHOCOLATE CAKE (CONTINUED)

COCONUT-PECAN FROSTING

½ cup (112 g) vegan butter

1 cup (200 g) sugar

1 tsp vanilla extract

1 (11.25-oz [332-ml]) can sweetened condensed coconut milk

3 large egg yolks, beaten

1½ cups (140 g) shredded coconut

1½ cups (165 g) chopped pecans

Prepare the frosting: In a medium-sized saucepan, melt the vegan butter over medium-low heat. Add the sugar, vanilla and condensed coconut milk and stir to combine. Drizzle in the egg yolks, making sure to whisk continuously as you add them. Bring to a simmer and cook for 21 to 25 minutes, stirring every 30 seconds, or until it thickens and turns golden. Remove from the heat and add the shredded coconut and chopped pecans. Stir to combine and allow the mixture to come to room temperature. If it sits for too long at room temperature, it will get a little hard, so once the cakes are cooled, frost immediately.

Place one-third of the frosting on one cake layer and spread evenly. Place a second layer on top and spread evenly with one-third of the frosting. Place the last layer on top and evenly spread the remaining frosting on top. I don't typically frost the sides of this.

Serve immediately or store in the fridge.

MY TWO-CENTS

You can get creative and use this chocolate cake with any frosting. I personally love the coconut-pecan frosting, and I can't get enough of it!

Alternatively, make 18 to 24 cupcakes instead of a layer cake: Bake for 17 minutes in a 350°F (180°C) oven, let cool completely, then frost.

FUNFETTI CAKE
WITH STRAWBERRY BUTTERCREAM

MAKES ONE
8" (20-CM)
2-LAYER CAKE

Coconut oil, for pans
1 cup (240 ml) water
1 cup (200 g) granulated sugar, divided
⅓ cup (75 g) vegan butter
2 tbsp (30 ml) melted coconut oil
1 cup (240 ml) coconut milk
2 large eggs
1 tbsp (15 ml) vanilla extract
Pinch of salt
2 tsp (9 g) baking soda
2 tsp (8 g) Paleo Grain-Free Baking Powder (page 231)
1 tsp xanthan gum
2½ cups (400 g) The Best Ever Gluten-Free All-Purpose Flour Blend (page 229)
¼ cup (40 g) multicolored sprinkles

Funfetti cake is a novelty recipe that we all remember loving and enjoying as children. You will be thrilled with how delicious and moist this simple gluten- and dairy-free version is to make. The strawberry buttercream is the perfect frosting for this fun and flavorful recipe.

Preheat the oven to 350°F (180°C). Oil two 8-inch (20-cm) round cake pans with coconut oil, then line the bottoms with parchment paper for easy removal.

In a medium-sized saucepan, combine the water with ½ cup (100) of the granulated sugar and bring to a low boil. Heat for 2 to 3 minutes, just until the sugar is dissolved. Remove from the heat and allow to cool.

In a stand mixer fitted with the paddle attachment, cream the remaining ½ cup (100 g) of granulated sugar with the butter and melted coconut oil on medium-low speed. Add the coconut milk and cooled water mixture. Add the eggs, vanilla, salt, baking soda, baking powder and xanthan gum. Allow to mix in for about 30 seconds, then add the flour blend, 1 cup (160 g) at a time, turning the mixer off to do this, if needed. Mix on medium speed for 3 to 4 minutes, scraping the sides of the bowl halfway through. The batter should have a slightly thick, creamy consistency. Fold in the sprinkles and mix them in gently.

Divide the batter evenly between the prepared pans. Bake for 25 to 30 minutes; a butter knife inserted into the center should come out completely clean.

Remove the cakes from the oven and let them cool in the pans for 20 minutes. Remove from the pans, transfer to a wire rack and let cool for at least 1 to 2 hours before frosting. You can refrigerate the layers and frost them the next day, or up to 2 days later.

(Continued)

FUNFETTI CAKE (CONTINUED)

STRAWBERRY BUTTERCREAM

½ cup (112 g) vegetable shortening

½ cup (112 g) vegan butter

3 cups (360 g) Grain-Free Powdered Sugar (page 230)

3 tbsp (45 ml) pureed strawberries (see note)

Prepare the buttercream: In the stand mixer fitted with the paddle attachment, cream the shortening and butter. Add the powdered sugar and mix on medium speed for 2 minutes. Scrape the sides of the bowl. Add the strawberry puree and mix on medium-high speed for 3 to 4 minutes, allowing the buttercream to fluff up.

To frost, place one-third of the frosting on one cake layer and spread evenly. Place a second layer on top and spread evenly with the remaining frosting. I don't typically frost the sides of this. If you would like to pipe decorations, you will need to double the frosting recipe.

MY TWO-CENTS

If you do not like coconut milk, any other nut milk will work well, too. You can use regular dairy products in this recipe if this does not need to be dairy-free.

To puree the strawberries, simply place them in a blender with a splash of water, if needed, and blend until smooth.

Feel free to use dye-free sprinkles, if you wish. Always make sure to check the ingredients for gluten, but if you need to be corn-free, too, make sure the sprinkles do not contain cornstarch or corn syrup.

Alternatively, make 18 to 24 cupcakes instead of a layer cake: Bake for 16 to 20 minutes in a 350°F (180°C) oven, let cool completely, then frost.

RED VELVET CAKE
WITH CREAM CHEESE BUTTERCREAM

MAKES ONE
8" (20-CM)
3-LAYER CAKE

Coconut oil, for pans
2 large eggs
1¼ cups (250 g) granulated sugar
½ cup (112 g) vegan butter
1 tsp vanilla extract
1 tsp white vinegar
1 cup (240 ml) coconut milk
1 tsp red food coloring
2 tsp (9 g) baking soda
2 tsp (8 g) Paleo Grain-Free Baking Powder (page 231)
½ tsp salt
1 tsp xanthan gum
2 tbsp (14 g) unsweetened cocoa powder
2½ cups (400 g) The Best Ever Gluten-Free All-Purpose Flour Blend (page 229)

CREAM CHEESE BUTTERCREAM

½ cup (112 g) vegan butter
2 (8-oz [225-g]) containers vegan cream cheese
1 tsp vanilla extract
5 cups (600 g) Grain-Free Powdered Sugar (page 230)

Rich, decadent red velvet cake is a true treat. It's fun to serve for special occasions, or to celebrate something. We often enjoy it for Easter. The light chocolate flavor with the cream cheese frosting is truly irresistible.

Preheat the oven to 350°F (180°C). Oil three 8-inch (20-cm) round cake pans with coconut oil.

In a stand mixer fitted with the paddle attachment, combine the eggs, granulated sugar and vegan butter. Mix on medium speed for 1 minute and then reduce the speed to low. Add the vanilla, white vinegar and coconut milk and blend for 30 seconds. While still mixing on low speed, add the red food coloring, baking soda, baking powder, salt, xanthan gum and cocoa powder. Increase the speed to medium and mix for 2 minutes, scraping the sides halfway through. Turn off the mixer and add the flour blend. Turn the mixer on at low speed and mix for 30 seconds, then increase the speed to medium and mix for 2 more minutes.

Divide the batter evenly among the prepared pans and bake on the middle rack for 14 to 16 minutes, or until a butter knife inserted into the center comes out clean.

Remove the cakes from the oven and let them cool in the pans for 20 minutes. Remove from the pans, transfer to a wire rack and let cool for at least 1 to 2 hours before frosting. You can refrigerate the layers and frost them the next day, or up to 2 days later.

Prepare the frosting: In the stand mixer, fitted with the paddle attachment, combine the vegan butter, vegan cream cheese and vanilla and mix on medium speed for 2 minutes. Scrape the sides and add 2 cups (240 g) of the powdered sugar, mix on medium-high speed for 1 minute and then reduce the speed to low. Beat in the remaining 3 cups (360 g) of powdered sugar, 1 cup (120 g) at a time. Once you have added all the powdered sugar, increase the mixer speed to high and mix for 2 minutes. The frosting should be fluffy and creamy.

To frost, place one-third of the frosting on one cake layer and spread evenly. Place a second layer on top and spread evenly with one-third of the frosting. Place the last layer on top and evenly spread the remaining frosting on top. I don't typically frost the sides of this. Serve, or store in the fridge.

PERFECT CARROT CAKE

While I was growing up, carrot cake was a dessert appreciated by my entire family. My grandparents especially love carrot cake. The last birthday cake I baked for my grandfather was a carrot cake, gluten-free of course. He passed a few months after that birthday, so this cake is very dear to me. It took me several years after his passing to make it again. After my family asked over and over for it, I decided to make it again and to share the recipe with you.

MAKES ONE 9 X 13" (23 X 33-CM) CAKE

Coconut oil, for pan
4 large eggs
2 tsp (10 ml) vanilla extract, divided
1 (18-oz [510-g]) can crushed pineapple, drained
½ cup (100 g) granulated sugar
1½ cups (338 g) light brown sugar
2 cups (220 g) shredded carrot
2 cups (186 g) shredded coconut, divided
¼ tsp ground cloves
1 tbsp (7 g) ground cinnamon
¼ tsp salt
1 cup (120 g) chopped walnuts, divided
1 cup (240 ml) melted coconut oil
2 tsp (8 g) Paleo Grain-Free Baking Powder (page 231)
1 tsp baking soda
1 tsp xanthan gum
2 cups (320 g) The Best Ever Gluten-Free All-Purpose Flour Blend (page 229)

CREAM CHEESE FROSTING

¼ cup (55 g) vegan butter
¼ cup (55 g) vegetable shortening
1 (8-oz [225-g]) container vegan cream cheese
2½ cups (300 g) Grain-Free Powdered Sugar (page 230)

Preheat the oven to 350°F (180°C). Oil a 9 x 13–inch (23 x 33–cm) baking pan with coconut oil.

In a stand mixer fitted with the paddle attachment, combine the eggs, 1 teaspoon vanilla, crushed pineapple, granulated and brown sugars and shredded carrot. Mix on medium-low speed for 1 minute. Add 1 cup (93 g) of shredded coconut and the cloves, cinnamon, salt and ½ cup (60 g) of chopped walnuts and blend for 30 seconds. Add the melted coco-nut oil and allow it to blend for 30 more seconds. Finally, add the baking powder, baking soda, xanthan gum and flour blend. Mix on medium speed for 3 minutes, scraping the sides of the bowl halfway through.

Pour the batter into the prepared baking pan and bake for 50 to 55 minutes, or until a butter knife inserted into the center comes out clean.

Remove the cake from the oven and let it cool in the pan for 20 minutes. Remove from the pan, transfer to a cooling rack and let cool for at least 1 to 2 hours before frosting. You can refrigerate the cake and frost it the next day or up to 2 days later.

Prepare the frosting: In a stand mixer fitted with the paddle attachment or in a medium-sized bowl, using a handheld mixer, cream the vegan butter, vegetable shortening, vegan cream cheese and remaining vanilla to a bowl. Add the powdered sugar, 1 cup (120 g) at a time, while blending on medium-high speed for 3 to 4 minutes, or until fluffy.

Frost the top of the cake once it has completely cooled, then evenly sprinkle the top with remaining chopped walnuts and shredded coconut. Store the cake in the fridge.

CHERRY PIE TARTLETS

I wait all year for cherries to come into season. I buy them in bulk, pit them and freeze them. Cherry pie is always something I make with the cherries. These tartlets are a fun and cute dessert when you want to impress guests or hand them out to friends.

MAKES 6 MINI PIES

2 tbsp (16 g) tapioca starch
¼ cup (60 ml) water
2 lb (905 g) pitted cherries
1 tbsp (15 ml) fresh lemon juice
1 tsp vanilla extract
1 cup (200 g) sugar
1 batch Easy Roll-Out Pie Dough (page 137)

Preheat the oven to 350°F (180°C). Have ready six 5-inch (12-cm)-diameter tartlet pans.

In a small bowl, combine the tapioca starch and water and stir until the starch dissolves.

In a medium-sized saucepan, combine the cherries, lemon juice, vanilla and sugar over medium heat. Stir well and then add the starch mixture. Bring to a boil, lower the heat and simmer, stirring every minute or so, for 8 to 10 minutes until the mixture thickens and the cherries are soft.

Roll out the pie dough to ¼ inch (6 mm) thick. Use a 4½-inch (11.5-cm)-diameter round cookie cutter to cut 6 disks, reserving the scraps, and place the rounds in the tartlet pans. Gently push the dough down into the pans until it shapes to the sides. Pour ½ cup (120 ml) of the filling into each tartlet shell. Reroll the remaining dough and cut ½-inch (1.3-cm)-wide strips to place over the top of the tartlets in a crisscross pattern.

Place the pans on a baking sheet and bake for 25 minutes, or until the crust is golden and the filling is bubbling.

Remove the tartlets from the oven and allow to cool for about 20 minutes before serving.

MY TWO-CENTS
Alternatively, you can make a single tart, in a 9-inch (23-cm) pie dish, instead of 6 tartlets, but you may need to increase the baking time by 10 to 15 minutes.

MASON JAR BANANA PUDDING PIES

MAKES 6 PUDDING PIES

PUDDING

½ cup (100 g) sugar

1 (13.5-oz [400-ml]) can coconut cream

1 cup (240 ml) coconut milk

2 tbsp (16 g) tapioca starch

1 large egg, beaten

1 tbsp (14 g) coconut oil

1 tbsp (15 ml) vanilla extract

CRUST

1 cup (90 g) gluten-free graham cracker crumbs, plus more for sprinkling (optional)

2 tbsp (30 ml) melted coconut oil

COCONUT WHIPPED CREAM

1 (13.5-oz [400-ml]) can coconut cream, refrigerated overnight

2 tsp (9 g) sugar

½ tsp vanilla extract

3 to 4 bananas (about 1 lb [455 g] total), sliced

This recipe was created out of nostalgia and because I wanted to share something with my children that I loved while growing up. Making the puddings in little Mason jars is superfun, and the best part is that you can easily pack them into lunches.

Have ready six 4-ounce (120-ml) Mason jars.

Prepare the pudding: In a large saucepan, combine the sugar, coconut cream, coconut milk and tapioca starch over medium-low heat. Cook, stirring the mixture constantly, for 3 to 4 minutes, or until all the coconut cream chunks are melted. Add the beaten egg while stirring the mixture. Continue to cook, stirring constantly, for 3 minutes; it should start to thicken. (If it is thickening very quickly, your heat is too high. Lower the heat slightly to slow it down.) Continue to cook, stirring once a minute, for about 10 minutes; it should come to a light boil. Allow it to simmer for 2 to 3 minutes more, then remove from the heat. Stir in the coconut oil and vanilla. Allow the pudding to come to room temperature.

Meanwhile, prepare the crust: In a medium-sized bowl, combine the graham cracker crumbs and melted coconut oil and mix with a fork. Add 2 tablespoons (about 11 g) of the crust mixture to the bottom of each Mason jar and press it down firmly with your fingers.

Prepare the coconut whipped cream: In a stand mixer fitted with the whisk attachment, combine only the cream from the can of coconut cream (you can save the water for smoothies) and the sugar. Start the mixer on low speed and add the vanilla. Increase the speed to high and whisk for 2 minutes. Turn off the mixer and scrape the sides. Turn the mixer back on and whisk on high speed for 4 more minutes. If the pudding has not cooled down by the time this is done, put the whipped mixture in the fridge to chill until you are ready to use it.

Once the pudding is completely cool, add a layer of sliced banana on top of the crust in the jars and then pour the pudding on top, distributing it evenly among the six jars. Add another layer of sliced banana, then the coconut whipped cream on top. Sprinkle with some graham cracker crumbs on top for decoration, if you would like. Chill the pies for at least an hour before serving, or store in the refrigerator until needed.

CHOCOLATE-COCONUT CREAM PIE

SERVES 8

1 batch Easy Roll-Out Pie Dough (page 137)

¾ cup (150 g) sugar

1 (13.5-oz [400-ml]) can coconut cream

2 cups (475 ml) coconut milk

½ cup (43 g) unsweetened cocoa powder

2 tbsp (16 g) tapioca starch

3 large egg yolks, beaten

2 tbsp (28 g) coconut oil

2 tsp (10 ml) vanilla extract

1 cup (85 g) shredded coconut

1 batch Coconut Whipped Cream (page 221), for topping

While growing up, we would eat the best chocolate cream pies from a local diner. This pie recipe is a fun twist on a traditional chocolate cream pie, but loaded with delicious coconut. My kiddos truly enjoy this pie and get really excited about it. The creamy chocolate center with a flaky buttery crust is a true treat.

Preheat the oven to 350°F (180°C).

Roll out the pie dough and fit into a 9-inch (23-cm) pie dish. Bake for 23 minutes, or until the crust is baked and lightly golden. Remove from the oven and allow to cool completely.

In a large saucepan, combine the sugar, coconut cream, coconut milk, cocoa powder and tapioca starch. Stir until well blended and place over medium-low heat. Cook for 4 minutes, stirring every 30 seconds. Slowly stir in the beaten egg yolks; the best way is to drizzle them in while stirring at the same time. Bring to a simmer and cook for 10 more minutes, stirring every minute. Remove from the heat and add the coconut oil and vanilla; stir to combine. Add the shredded coconut and stir well to incorporate.

Allow the pudding to cool down to room temperature, then pour it into the cooled pie shell. Refrigerate overnight and serve topped with the coconut whipped cream.

MY TWO-CENTS
Save the egg whites from the 3 eggs and make the Bakery-Style French Bread (page 145) with them.

NO-BAKE VEGAN LEMON CHEESECAKE

I love no-bake desserts! This simple recipe is quick to throw together with minimal ingredients. The lemon flavor shines and everyone will love and enjoy this delicious cheesecake. Feel confident serving this to your family and friends who are not gluten-free.

CRUST

1½ cups (135 g) crushed gluten-free cookies (see note)

3 tbsp (45 ml) melted coconut oil

FILLING

1 (13.5-oz [400-ml]) can coconut cream

1 (8-oz [225-g]) container vegan cream cheese

¾ cup (150 g) sugar

Zest and juice of 1 lemon

Lemon zest and slices, for garnish (optional)

Prepare the crust: In a medium-sized bowl, combine the crushed cookies and the melted coconut oil. Stir with a fork until well incorporated.

Pour the cookie mixture into an ungreased 9-inch (23-cm) springform pan. Spread out evenly and push the crust mixture down to create a tight, flat crust. Set aside.

Prepare the filling: In a blender, combine the coconut cream, cream cheese, sugar and lemon zest and juice. Blend on medium speed for about 1 minute, or until well mixed and creamy.

Pour the filling over the crust and freeze overnight.

Remove from the freezer 20 minutes before serving, to allow the cheesecake to soften. Garnish with lemon zest and slices, if desired.

This needs to be stored in the freezer.

MY TWO-CENTS

Any crushed cookie or graham cracker will work for the crust (check their ingredients if you need them to be corn- or dairy-free); I used a food processor to crush them.

You may use heavy cream and regular cream cheese, if this does not need to be dairy-free or vegan.

NO-BAKE VEGAN CHOCOLATE CHEESECAKE

This is the perfect dessert for hot weather. The filling is supersimple: You just throw the ingredients in a blender and then pour. I love serving this to guests because it can be made the night before and taken out a few minutes before serving. The vegan cream cheese makes it rich.

SERVES 8

VEGAN

CRUST

1½ cups (135 g) crushed gluten-free cookies (see note)

3 tbsp (45 ml) melted coconut oil

FILLING

1 (8-oz [225-g]) container vegan cream cheese

1 (15-oz [444-ml]) can coconut cream

¾ cup (65 g) unsweetened cocoa powder

¾ cup (150 g) sugar

1 tsp vanilla extract

CHOCOLATE GANACHE

1 cup (175 g) vegan chocolate chips

1 tbsp (14 g) coconut oil

Prepare the crust: In a bowl, combine the crushed cookies and melted coconut oil. Blend well and pour into an ungreased 9-inch (23-cm) springform pan. Spread out evenly and push the crust mixture down to create a tight, flat crust. Set aside.

Prepare the filling: In a blender, combine the cream cheese, coconut cream, cocoa powder, sugar and vanilla. Blend for about a minute, stop the blender and stir the mixture around with a spatula, and then blend again until nice and creamy.

Pour the filling on top of the crust and freeze overnight.

Remove from the freezer 20 minutes before serving.

Meanwhile, prepare the ganache: In a small saucepan, combine the chocolate chips and coconut oil. Heat over medium-low heat, stirring, until melted, about 3 minutes. Remove from the heat immediately and allow to cool for about 5 minutes.

Pour the ganache onto the top of the cheesecake and spread, if needed. Allow it to set for about 15 minutes and then serve. You can put it in the fridge to help it set, if needed.

MY TWO-CENTS

You can use any cookies to make the crust (check their ingredients if you need them to be corn- or dairy-free); I used a food processor to crush them.

Top with your favorite fruit, if desired.

You can use regular cream cheese and heavy cream if this does not need to be dairy-free or vegan.

Basic Essentials

These recipes are my essentials for gluten-free cooking and baking. Because my son is corn-free I also need to have corn-free baking powder and powdered sugar. You can purchase these items, but they are not always easy to find and are usually very costly. In this chapter, you will find my gluten-free all-purpose flour recipe (page 229), which I highly recommend when you are baking from this book or any gluten-free recipe. This simple blend is all I have used for my gluten-free baking since 2012, when I created this recipe.

THE BEST EVER GLUTEN-FREE ALL-PURPOSE FLOUR BLEND

MAKES 6 CUPS (960 G) FLOUR BLEND

4 cups (640 g) brown rice flour
1 cup (128 g) tapioca starch
1 cup (192 g) potato starch

Having a gluten-free all-purpose flour blend that works is essential for successful baking. Not all blends are created equal and most are very expensive. I created this blend to give everyone the opportunity to enjoy delicious gluten-free food. You can find these ingredients in all major stores, and it is inexpensive to make. Most important—it works!

In a bowl, combine all the ingredients and blend well. Store in an airtight container.

MY TWO-CENTS
I usually double this. It stores well in the pantry for about 8 weeks.

GRAIN-FREE POWDERED SUGAR

MAKES
1½ CUPS (200 G)
POWDERED SUGAR

1 cup (200 g) sugar
1 tbsp (8 g) tapioca starch

Most store-bought powdered sugar contains corn. When we found out about my son's corn allergy, I found it difficult to find a commercial brand without corn that was affordable. This is easy to make and much less expensive than purchasing from the store.

In a high-powered blender, combine the sugar and tapioca starch. Blend on high speed until the mixture has a powdered sugar consistency.

MY TWO-CENTS
After blending, allow the blender to sit with the lid on for about 10 minutes. It needs time to settle, otherwise a lot of it will fly out the top when you take off the lid.

PALEO GRAIN-FREE BAKING POWDER

MAKES 4⅓ TABLESPOONS (54 G) BAKING POWDER

3 tbsp (41 g) baking soda
1 tbsp (10 g) cream of tartar
1 tsp tapioca starch

My son has a mild corn allergy, and when I realized that baking powder contained corn, we needed a safe alternative. This is my go-to recipe for all of our baking. It is great for Paleo and grain-free recipes, too.

In a small bowl, combine all the ingredients and stir well. Store in a Mason jar.

MY TWO-CENTS
I like to double this recipe. Any starch will work in place of tapioca starch. This can harden over time, so stir it often and before use.

SIMPLE FROM-SCRATCH MAYO

This Whole30/Paleo mayo is a staple recipe that I make often to use for ranch, or just to smother on my food. It's incredibly easy to make and doesn't contain the extra junk most store-bought mayo does.

In a medium-sized Mason jar, combine all the ingredients and use an immersion blender to blend until thick and creamy. Store in the fridge for up to 1 week.

MAKES 1½ CUPS (337 G) MAYO

PALEO, WHOLE30

1 cup (240 ml) avocado oil
1 large egg
1 tsp salt
½ tsp dry mustard
1 tbsp (15 ml) fresh lemon juice

MY TWO-CENTS
You can use olive oil in place of the avocado, and cider vinegar in place of the lemon juice.

Make sure to measure the lemon juice precisely.

Don't be alarmed if the color is slightly yellow if using olive oil; the dark color of the oil can give the mayo a slight yellow color.

Tips and Tricks

ACTIVATING YEAST

To make superfluffy breads and baked goods, yeast is often involved. A lot of people can be intimidated by activating yeast and dealing with it—I was at first. After doing it a couple of times, it feels like second nature, so I encourage you to jump in and do it.

To activate yeast, you will need warm water, and on some occasions, warm milk. The perfect temperature for this is 110°F (43°C). I suggest purchasing a candy thermometer; you can get them anywhere, and you will need to know the temperature of many things you are cooking, so it's worth getting. How I usually activate the yeast is to boil the water and then pour the amount the recipe calls for into a 4-cup (1-L) Pyrex measuring cup. I let it come to temperature, then add the sugar and yeast and give it a quick stir. Once the yeast doubles in size, it is activated and ready to use.

ROLLING OUT DOUGH

Rolling out gluten-free dough can be extremely difficult. A lot of gluten-free doughs are sticky, which is done on purpose to create a good texture. Most of the time, the dough is too sticky for parchment paper and will stick as you peel away the paper. I have found that for rolling out all of my doughs, I need to use plastic wrap. It peels perfectly! To do this, I line my work surface with plastic wrap. I will often have to use two sheets so it covers my entire working surface. I place the dough on top and then more plastic wrap on top of that. I then roll my dough between the two pieces of plastic wrap. If it sticks to your surface slightly, as in doesn't want to come up without losing shape, then simply grab the corner of the plastic wrap and pull up; this loosens it from the wrap and makes it much easier to remove.

PREPARING THE PAN

Through the years, I have found the best pan preparer to be coconut oil. I have tried using vegan butter, nonstick spray and even flouring the pan as I was taught while growing up, but nothing works as well as coconut oil. When I bake my cakes and breads, I always generously oil the pan with coconut oil and everything pops right out.

Tools for Success

CANDY THERMOMETER

I use this all the time. It is essential for monitoring the temperature of your oil when you are frying such things as donuts, apple fritters and onion rings. I also use it to make sure my water is the perfect temperature for activating yeast.

COOKIE DOUGH SCOOP/ICE-CREAM SCOOP

These are always great to have on hand and are not just for cookies and ice cream. I listed both because sometimes people get the two mixed up. A cookie scoop is much smaller than an ice-cream scoop and literally makes the prettiest perfect cookies. I use my ice-cream scooper for such things as biscuits, scones and even the topping for the Southern-Style Peach Cobbler (page 192).

DUTCH OVEN

I use my Dutch oven so often that it has earned a place on top of the stove. I use this for roasts, frying foods and so much more. They are great and if you can swing it, a Le Creuset is a fabulous investment.

ELECTRIC WINE OPENER

Well, need I say more? We all need a good glass of wine while we are working away in the kitchen, and this tool is great.

HIGH-SPEED BLENDER

I recently got one and it has been a game changer. You can get by with a regular blender, but a great high-speed one allows you to do a lot more and to make supercreamy sauces.

IMMERSION BLENDER

This is my go-to for making mayonnaise or for blending soup in the pot to make it creamy.

MARBLE ROLLING PIN AND MARBLE PASTRY BLOCK

If you have granite (or natural stone) countertops, you don't need one, but if you have tile countertops like me, then a flat, cold surface is essential for rolling out dough.

MEAT THERMOMETER

This is a must for every cook who cooks meat. I use it for whole chickens, steak, roasts and when grilling.

PIZZA CUTTER

You will use this for more than just cutting pizza. I use it for cutting Cherry Hand Pies (page 162), the top of the Cherry Pie Tartlets (page 218) and so much more.

SPIDER STRAINER

This is essentially a metal basket with a wooden handle. This is what you need for frying food and also what I use when boiling bagels and bagel dogs. I use this often.

STAND MIXER

A good stand mixer is an investment, but truly worth it. I have had mine since I went gluten-free, and it has been such a huge part of my daily life. You will see in most recipes that I have specified to use a stand mixer. If you plan on doing a lot of cooking, I truly suggest getting one.

Thankful

I am so thankful to so many for loving and supporting me while I wrote this book. It truly does take a village.

First, I would like to thank Page Street Publishing for allowing me to make this masterpiece and for supporting me through it!

Thank you to my husband, James, for taking the time to read through all the recipes and taste test everything. Without you and your support, I could never have done this! You are my rock, partner and best friend. I could never imagine walking this journey without you by my side.

Thank you to my babies James and Claire; your love keeps me going! You think our house is a bakery, and because of that, you are so incredibly picky. I love that you want to be in the kitchen with me, learning and making huge messes. Forgive me when I am stressed and short-tempered when I am working. I am so blessed to have both of you to love every day.

Grandma Olga, thank you for your recipe box, plus all your love and support. Your recipes are always my favorite, and I still love it when you cook for me. Being in the kitchen with you as a child are my favorite childhood memories.

Thank you to my best friend Jennifer. You helped me brainstorm through it all and come up with the recipes. Your photography help and expertise, editing advice and taste tasting truly helped me to create this book. I love you and I am so lucky that you are my best friend and sister.

Thank you to my aunt Julie, aunt Cheryl and cousins for helping with the kids! Thank you for your love, the recipes you shared with me and the beautiful memories you gave me as a child.

Thank you to my mom, Jerri, for loving my kiddos and taking over when I needed to work. You are always there for me, and I couldn't have done any of this without you and your support.

Thank you to my little sister Jewell. I will not make that mistake again! I love you, Tera!

A huge thanks to my Freely readers who keep coming back, loving and supporting me. I do this for you!

About the Author

Jennifer Bigler is a wife, mother and part of a food allergy family. She is the blogger behind the popular blog Living Freely Gluten Free. With a love for creation, she is always in the kitchen. After going gluten-free she was determined to re-create all of the foods she loved and craved. Being a member of a food allergy family has made her have to get very creative and experiment to make the recipes safe for her entire family. She has been featured in the *Gluten Free Times* and *Seattle Refined* magazine and was voted one of the top 20 gluten-free bloggers of 2017. She believes in sharing all of the gluten-free goodness and through this book wants to get everyone back in the kitchen enjoying the foods they love with the people they love!

Index